Architectural
Lighting Design

A PRACTICAL GUIDE

Architectural Lighting Design

A PRACTICAL GUIDE

Admir Jukanović

THE CROWOOD PRESS

First published in 2018 by
The Crowood Press Ltd
Ramsbury, Marlborough
Wiltshire SN8 2HR

enquiries@crowood.com

www.crowood.com

This impression 2022

British Library Cataloguing-in-Publication Data
A catalogue record for this book is available from the British Library.

ISBN 978-1-78500-457-5

Typeset by Servis Filmsetting Ltd, Stockport, Cheshire
Printed and bound by CPI Group (UK) Ltd, Croydon, CR0 4YY

Contents

Beauty is revealed by light and the delicate play between light, shade and colour. When correctly applied, good artificial architectural lighting has a natural quality that instinctively feels right and helps us to feel good. The need for lighting design rather than lighting that fulfils the regulatory and statutory requirements began half a century ago.

ARCHITECTURAL LIGHTING DESIGN BEGAN to get noticed in the 1950s in the United States and later spilled over to the UK and some other European countries. Lighting design is a fairly new job description. There aren't many courses to enroll in if one wants to become a lighting designer. Not being able to influence what is taught in the few courses available leads many lighting design consultancies to educate their own future lighting designers. In fact, some consultancies prefer to foster their own talent to assure a good-quality basic training paired with a design philosophy that matches the company's philosophy. Many lighting designers have either a design or architecture background and received their basic education and finishing at a consultancy. I myself am a product of this process and all I know has either been learned on the job or self-taught. Now, I have started to share my knowledge and experience with the newcomers arriving at our consultancy.

This book is aimed at all new starters and the interested alike, and will hopefully become a foundation for architects and future lighting designers. Therefore, this book covers the technical aspects of lighting design as much as design-related features. The structure of the book allows a person not familiar with lighting to get a step-by-step introduction to lighting design. It starts with the basics of lamps and luminaires and the lighting tools available. These three first chapters form the technical groundwork of the book. The fourth chapter is the core of the book and explores the key aspects of lighting design, while the fifth chapter demonstrates what deliverables are expected and how to present them. All explanations are backed up by images and diagrams throughout, though most of the architectural images used in this book have been saved for the final chapter. Rather than finishing with case studies of successfully executed jobs, this book closes with pitfalls, as a successful lighting design scheme depends as much on well-executed details and the avoidance of pitfalls as it does on its overarching concept.

This book will not teach you how to be creative and come up with a great lighting concept, but it does offer the tools and advice to create the structure of knowledge and the safety net you undoubtedly will need to do so.

Chapter 1

THE BASICS – LAMPS

BEFORE GETTING INTO THE BASIS OF ARTIficial lighting, the so-called light source, let's take a brief look at its terminology. What most people don't know is that what normal people call a bulb is actually a lamp. Mind you, most of the lamps used today do not come in bulbous shapes anymore but are available in various shapes from the tube to the sphere to the cone. Each light source, whether fluorescent, gas-discharge, LED or incandescent, should ideally be called a lamp.

Fig. 1.02 A luminaire by the Artemide.

Fig. 1.01 Different types of lamps.

THE LUMINAIRE

To make things more confusing, people not involved in the lighting industry call a light fixture a lamp. When the oil light fixture got replaced by the safer and brighter gas light fixture and then by the safer and brighter electric incandescent light fixture people understandably decided to call it 'the lamp' only. In the lighting industry, however, it is still called the light fixture, light fitting or, more elegantly, the luminaire.

ALL ABOUT EFFICIENCY

Since the invention of the practical electric incandescent lamp by Swan/Edison in 1878/1879, many improvements have taken place. Lamps have either become more efficient or smaller or have a greater life expectancy. However, the improvement of one aspect of the light source doesn't mean all the attributes have improved. Whilst some lamps improved in life expectancy and efficiency they lost the capacity to be dimmed. Being able to differentiate between the various parameters of each lamp is crucial when working and designing with light.

One of the most important parameters defining the quality of a lamp is its efficiency. Due to the introduction of the electric meter reader, rising electricity prices and increased ecological awareness the efficiency of lamps has become ever more important. The following explanations should help you to understand what defines the efficiency of a light source.

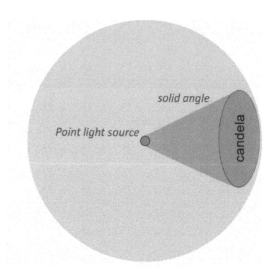

Fig. 1.03 Luminous intensity – areal intensity.

Wattage

We all know that a watt is a power unit and that more wattage means more power for a light source. So, if one wants a brighter light source, knowing the wattage helps to quantify the light output. The light output increases with an increasing wattage. Therefore, a higher wattage seems to be better and should give more light. This, however, applies only when comparing apples to apples. For example, a 35w metal halide lamp produces more light than a 100w incandescent lamp. Knowing the wattage does not allow us to compare the light quantity of various light sources. We need to take a look at another aspect of the light source as well.

Luminous intensity: (areal intensity)

The intensity of a light is best defined by its luminous intensity. Luminous intensity of emitted light is measured in candela. This reveals the concentration of emitted light per second by a light source shining in one direction and at a solid angle. It takes into consideration only the wave spectrum our eyes are capable of processing.

Lumens: (overall intensity)

The second parameter is the lumens output. If one wants to know how much light a lamp emits, one has to know how much lumen it produces. Lumen is a measure for all the visible light emitted by a light source. These figures are very useful as they give us an indication of how much light a lamp emits in total or what overall output one can expect from a lamp. It is still not enough to evaluate the efficiency of a light source, however, as it doesn't include the energy or the wattage used in achieving this output.

Fig. 1.04 Luminous intensity – overall intensity.

Luminous efficacy

Here the luminous efficacy comes in as it defines the lumens per watt a light source emits. This is probably the best way to compare apples to oranges as it reduces every light source to a basic efficacy ratio. Now we can compare the efficacy of any light source. We can compare the light output of an incandescent lamp of 16lm/w with a state-of-the-art LED light source producing 100lm/w.

Natural light or an artificial light with a CRI 100 refracted by a prism.

Artificial light with a low CRI refracted by a prism.

Fig. 1.06a Natural light or an artificial light with a CRI 100 refracted by a prism.

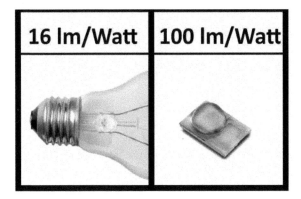

Fig. 1.05 Luminous efficacy.

ALL ABOUT QUALITY

Despite its many appealing features, one cannot say that an LED light is in all aspects superior to an incandescent light source. The light produced by incandescent lamps is, in most cases, perceived as 'more natural' and these lamps reproduce colours with more depth and intensity than other light sources. As a matter of fact, the incandescent lamp acts together with daylight as our benchmark when it comes to natural light colour reproduction. There are a few LED modules that can mimic and exceed incandescent lamps in CRI.

Colour Rendition Index (CRI)

Until the introduction of replacements for the incandescent lamp we didn't have to pay attention to colour rendition. The incandescent light source produced a light perceived as warm and natural. The colours lit by the incandescent lamp appeared true when compared with a natural light. Shortly after the first incandescent replacements were introduced, people started to realize that the quality of the light did not match Edison's/Swan's original or natural light. The colours lit by the replacements appeared duller and flatter. The best way to visualize and understand this is to compare the light that different lamps produce by analysing their emitted light spectrum. While incandescent light, when split by a prism, produces a continuous spectrum of light colours, fluorescent light is able to produce only an interrupted, incomplete light colour spectrum. Its colour rendition is compromised accordingly as it lacks elements of the light spectrum that allow it to reveal colour accurately.

The colour rendition of a fluorescent lamp or high-pressure sodium light sources is low when compared to the ideal natural light. The Colour Rendition Index (CRI) has been introduced so we can measure the capacity of a light source to display colours faithfully when compared to a natural or ideal light source. The ideal or best CRI is 100 and is reproduced by natural light, incandescent lamps or halogen lamps. All trustworthy manufacturers are

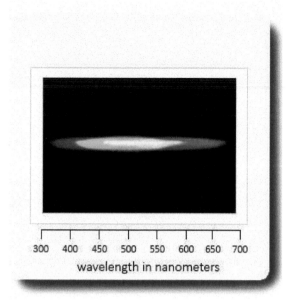

Fig. 1.06b Light diffraction with a 35mm (1.4in) slide to evaluate the colour rendition of a light source.

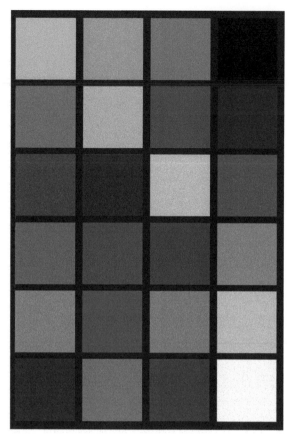

Fig. 1.07 Colour rendition chart.

able to present the CRI of their product. If this is not the case, one should refrain from specifying the light source. There are, however, various methods to check a light source's colour renditions. The numeric CRI value can't be verified like this, but this kind of checking nevertheless allows for a subjective comparison and evaluation.

One could buy an expensive light meter that can provide an accurate colour rendition graph, but the easiest and most cost-effective way to test colour rendition is to consider a lamp with a spectroscope, which one holds against the light's source.

Light passes through the foil, creating all visible spectral light colours. If it shows all spectral colours, the colour rendition is good while a lower colour rendition will produce gaps in some of the areas. This approach shows the colour wave length the light is lacking but not the effect it has on colours. This can be checked with a colour checker also called a colour rendition chart.

A colour checker allows one to see how colours will look under the light sources they are exposed to. It is a black card board with twenty-four coloured squares mounted onto it. The colour checker contains a representation of colours from real objects, such as skin or foliage to primary, secondary, miscellaneous and greyscale colours.

If all colours are shown correctly when compared with an ideal light source, the rendition can be considered as good. Originally introduced to verify correct lighting in photography and movie-making it is also increasingly used today by critical lighting professionals as benchmark chart.

Colour temperature

When entering a DIY shop to try and buy a white paint one realizes quickly that there is no single white on display but a variety of whites. One realizes quickly that the shopping might take a bit longer than anticipated as the decision about which white to paint our

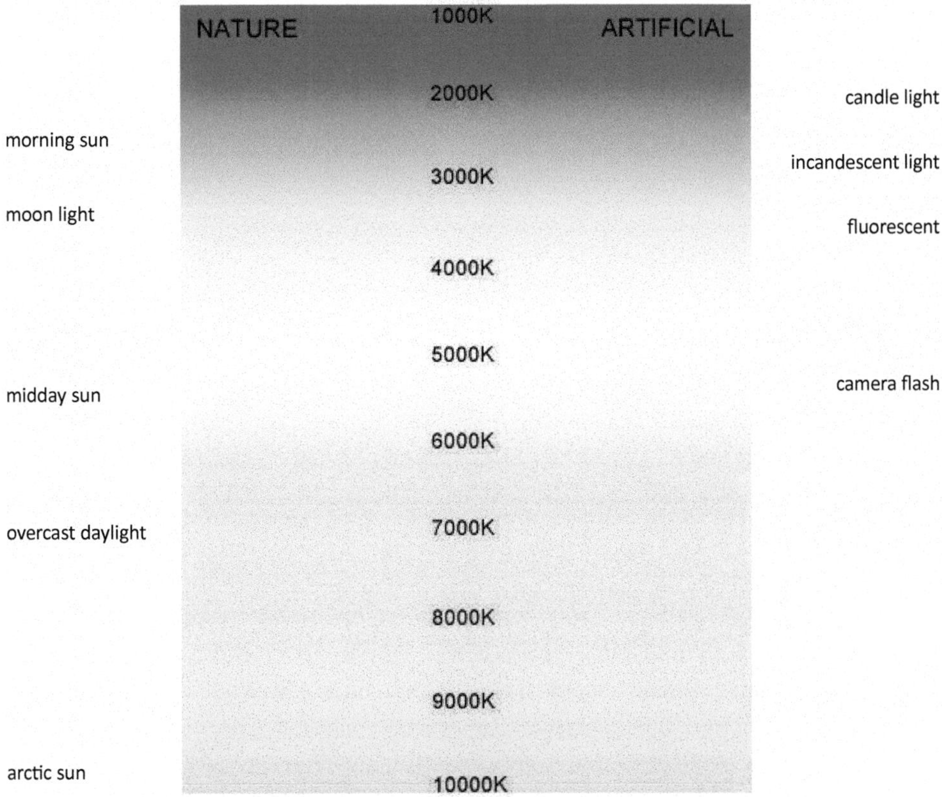

NATURE	1000K	ARTIFICIAL
	2000K	candle light
morning sun	3000K	incandescent light
moon light		fluorescent
	4000K	
	5000K	
midday sun		camera flash
	6000K	
overcast daylight	7000K	
	8000K	
	9000K	
arctic sun	10000K	

Fig. 1.08 Colour temperature scale.

walls with is, of course, important to us. The same applies to white light sources. There is no single white light source in a shop display but a variety of white light colours and it is important that the white light one chooses feels right. The colour temperature of white light is measured in kelvins and ranges from the warm 1700K of a candle to the cold bluish 20000K of the arctic sky. Our sun is a great example of the variance of white light. The sun emits in the morning and evening a warm white light, creating visually warm surfaces. The light gets increasingly cold, reaching its peak when the sun is at its highest point in the sky.

Artificial light sources seek to mimic daylight and are available in all colour temperatures. They start from a very warm 2400K and usually end with the cold 6500K. The colour temperature 4000K is perceived as neutral white, neither assignable to the warm spectrum of white light nor to the cold spectrum.

Colour temperature preferences

The preferences towards colour temperature vary from country to country. In northern countries, warm light is generally the preferred choice. A warm light seems more inviting in a region dominated by cold nights and days throughout the years. In southern countries however, the opposite is the case. In a warm climate, a cold light invites you to cool down and refresh and is therefore the generally preferred choice.

Of course, this is not to say that there are not variations across West and East as well as cultural exceptions.

Fig. 1.09 Warm, inviting light, Kakslauttanen Arctic Resort.

Colour temperature and objects

To cast an object or a product in the right light, not only is a good colour rendition important but also the right colour temperature. The appearance of an object changes with the colour temperature it is exposed to. Some colour temperatures are more suitable for some objects than other. This knowledge must be taken in consideration when choosing a lamp. Products like meat profit from more reddish warm light whereas fruits look best in bright neutral daylight. Bread products look best in a warm orange light whereas fish will look fresh and appealing under bright cool light.

The coverage of the exposition area is important. When we buy meat and fish we like to see the entire product. These items usually can't be touched by us before purchase; therefore, we rely almost completely on our visual senses. We are particularly sensitive when purchasing them and do not appreciate when some parts of the products are left in darkness. Bread, on the other hand, comes daily into our bakeries and we touch it through the packaging to test whether it is soft inside and crispy outside. Here, lighting is allowed to be more dramatic. Partial light is more forgiving, and so should be used in display areas where possible, such as in bakeries where full lighting is not essential.

Light distribution

When illuminating objects, the distribution chosen is important. Lamps distribute light differently. Fluorescent lamps and LED tubes, for example, generate a diffuse soft light with a big emission surface while incandescent, halogen and metal halide light sources, and their LED counterparts, emit light from a small point, creating strong shadows. In both cases, the distribution is almost 360 degrees but the effect caused is different.

In the early days of artificial lighting, these light sources were either used bare or behind a shade. However, soon, the first light sources would be used with an external reflector, allowing one to guide the light at the angle and in the direction needed. Lamp manufacturers have quickly learned to integrate reflectors and offer various point-light sources with

Fig. 1.10 Colour temperature in relation to products.

Reddish white light	Cold and bright light	Warm light
MEAT	**FISH**	**BREAD**

Available in beam angle of 6-60 degrees. Creating a directional and defined light with very strong shadows on lit objects.	Point source with a light distribution of almost 360 degrees. Creating a multi-directional and defined light with strong shadows on lit objects.	Linear diffused light source. Creating a multi-directional soft light with soft shadows.

Fig. 1.11 Light distribution of various lamps.

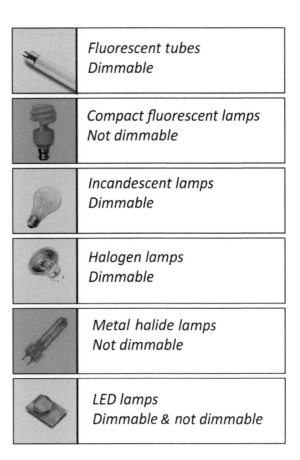

Fig. 1.12 Dimmability chart.

integral reflectors forcing the light into a specific angle. The so-called beam angle is important as it spreads light very precisely, allowing one to illuminate some areas very strongly while leaving others in darkness.

Many luminaires come with reflectors; others, however, allow the usage of lamps with integrated reflectors. This permits one to change the distribution of the light after the luminaire has been installed by simply changing the lamp rather than the entire light fitting.

Dimmability

As the day changes, light intensity changes, and so does our need for artificial light. At home, we would like to use one and the same luminaire to either fill our living room with light or to create a subtle and soft light. In a theatre play, dimming and tuning lights is essential as this allows us to gradually withdraw attention from one side of the stage, moving it slowly to the other. Besides changing the mood, dimming light can serve the cause of saving energy by supplying only the light needed rather than the full amount of light available. This has in most cases the positive side effect of extending the life expectancy of the light source considerably. Not all light sources are dimmable. Some lamp groups allow full dimmability while others cannot be dimmed at all. Lighting designers tend to use dimmable lamp types in interior projects as they allow the change of light scenes and precise light-level adjustment. Dimmability unfortunately has its price. Therefore, choosing when to go for dimmable lamps and when to use only non-dimmable light sources depends often on a project's budget as much as it depends on the project's requirements.

Life expectancy

The life expectancy of a light source might not be an issue when replacing a desk light equipped with

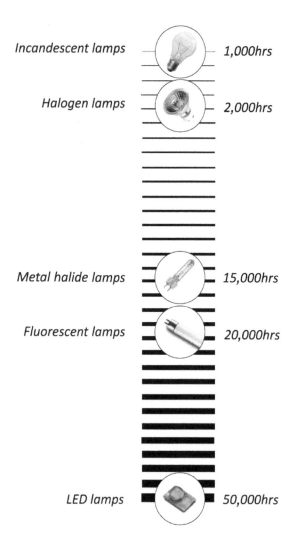

Incandescent lamps		1,000hrs
Halogen lamps		2,000hrs
Metal halide lamps		15,000hrs
Fluorescent lamps		20,000hrs
LED lamps		50,000hrs

Fig. 1.13 Life expectancy.

a low voltage halogen lamp. The price of the replacement lamp is affordable. The desk lamp might be used on average only one hour daily. This means that with an average life expectancy of 2,000 hours it needs replacing every five and a half years. It is usually a very simple process as there are no special tools required and it can be done while sitting on the office chair at home.

The viewpoint changes dramatically when changing lamps in a ten-storey-high atrium or in a huge office building where more than 1,000 lamps are used ten hours daily at three-metre height. The life expectancy of a lamp suddenly becomes one of the prime

factors. Life expectancy varies between 2,000 hours and 50,000 hours, and a lighting system is only as good as its weakest link. Besides the lamp, one has to take the ballasts and their operating hours into consideration.

The lamp property star

When specifying luminaires and their lamps for a project, one will automatically ask for certain properties of a light source. When choosing a lamp and the light it produces, one usually divides its properties into aesthetic properties and numeric properties.

First, the subjective or aesthetic light quality a lamp delivers is chosen. Colour rendition, colour temperature and the light distribution create what one could call an aesthetic triangle as they define the aesthetic properties of the lamp. On the other hand, elements that are not directly related to the aesthetic perception of the light, like its dimmability, life expectancy and efficiency form the second basic triangle. Together, these triangles form a lamp property star that might help you to ask the right questions when looking for the right lamp for a project.

Fig. 1.14 Lamp property star.

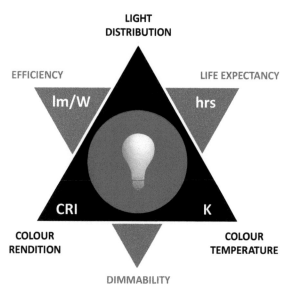

TRADITIONAL LAMP TYPES

We are at an exciting stage in lighting design as we are experiencing a lighting revolution. The LED is able to replace most of the lamps we manufacture today. It is only a matter of time before it will replace all known light sources. What hinders it currently are two key factors: the price and the fact that there are many luminaires out there that still work with the old lamps. The LED manufacturers offer alternatives for these lamps and are able to cover most of the lamp replacements needed for the market. However, it is still worth taking a look at the existing 'old' light sources. Why? Well, firstly, we are still in a transition period and it will take some time before all lamps are replaced by LEDs. Secondly, as LED manufacturers are aiming to replace existing lamps, one should understand whether they are really replacing an apple with an apple. A lighting designer should be able to evaluate an LED replacement. To do so, one needs to understand the three main lamp groups, their functions and their attributes.

Incandescent lamps

It all started with the bulb-shaped incandescent lamp so let's start with it as well. The incandescent lamp is to many people a well-known old companion, first mass produced in its current shape by Thomas Edison in the 1880s. The principle behind it is simple and is based on temperature radiation. A thin, curled, vacuum-sealed carbon filament heats up and starts to emit light when a current is applied. The higher the current, the higher the light emission.

Soon, inventors all over the world started to look for improvements. Tungsten metal, also known as wolfram, proved to be a superior filament and replaced the carbon filament. The vacuum originally preventing the filament from oxidation got filled with

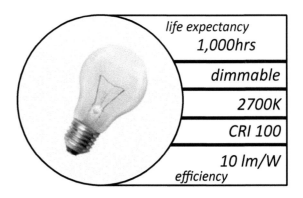

Fig. 1.15 Lamp properties – GLS incandescent lamp.

halogen which again improved the performance of the lamps. Mass production and the cheap pricing of incandescent lamps made them spread quickly. They come in all shapes and sizes and became the prime domestic light source throughout the twentieth century. Unfortunately, this method of generating light is inefficient and produces mostly heat. The fragile and thin filament usually stops working after 1,000–2,000 hours and less than 5 per cent of the energy input is transformed into light. Therefore, many countries are now banning common incandescent lamps, also called GLS lamps, from the market. However, we might continue to see tungsten halogen lamps due to their higher efficiency in the years ahead.

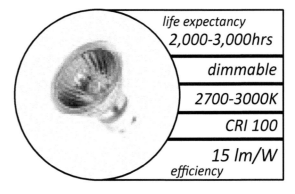

Fig. 1.16 Lamp properties – halogen lamp.

Metal halide lamps

While the incandescent lamp emits lights through heat radiation, the metal halide lamp generates light by creating an electric arc. To do so, it requires two electrodes and a mixture of metal halides contained under high pressure. The bright light is generated when the arc vaporizes the halides within the so-called arc tube. The second tube around the arc tube prevents heat loss and is often used to control the emission of UV (ultraviolet) light. High-intensity gas discharge lamps need time to reach their desired light intensity and once turned off require time to cool down and to be able to reignite. Metal halide cannot be dimmed. To run metal halide lamps, one requires an external ballast to provide the needed ignition and to control the current. On the other hand, metal halide lamps do have a good colour rendition and are highly efficient, with a life expectancy of up to 15,000 hours. Therefore, they were widely used in the retail sector and in many public buildings as well as in street lighting and for stadium illumination.

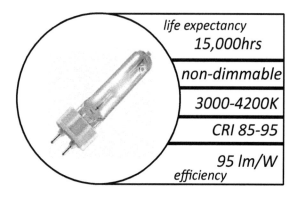

life expectancy
15,000hrs

non-dimmable

3000-4200K

CRI 85-95

95 lm/W
efficiency

Fig. 1.17 Lamp properties – metal halide lamp.

Fluorescent lamps

Fluorescent lamps are low-pressure gas discharge lamps. They are in effect a glass tube filled predominately with argon and a small quantity of mercury. At each end, they contain coated tungsten filament cathodes that emit electrons when put under current. A high-voltage pulse moves the electrons through the tube creating an argon arc. The arc vaporizes the mercury within the tube, producing UV light. All fluorescent lamps are coated with phosphor that emits visible light once energized by the UV light. The composition of the phosphor defines what colour temperature the light is going to have. Unlike an incandescent lamp and the high-intensity gas discharge lamp, the fluorescent lamp does not get hot. Beside the standard tube-shaped fluorescent lamp, there is the compact fluorescent lamp that is found more frequently in households than its relatives. Unlike the tube-shaped fluorescent lamps that are run with a remote electronic control gear, the compact fluorescent lamps have an integrated control gear that allows them to be used off the shelf and screwed into standard fixtures. Just like the metal halide lamp, the compact fluorescent lamp it is a true workhorse: efficient and with a high life expectancy. Therefore, it can still be found nearly everywhere from office buildings to galleries and in our homes. The CRI is lower than in incandescent and metal halide lamps but it has an impressive efficiency that lies at around 20 per cent. It lasts around 20,000 hours, significantly longer than an incandescent lamp.

It also emits less heat; therefore, its surface is touchable. Unfortunately, fluorescent lamps contain highly toxic mercury and require specific waste management as they need to be separated from your general waste.

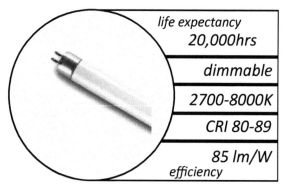

life expectancy
20,000hrs

dimmable

2700-8000K

CRI 80-89

85 lm/W
efficiency

Fig. 1.18 Lamp properties – fluorescent lamp.

LAMP CONNECTION METHOD

Lamp types do come in different sizes and shapes. Throughout the decades, different connection methods have developed and become standards. Screw connections are probably the one most known to all of us. E27 and E14 screw sockets hold standard Edison incandescent lamps and haven't changed since Edison launched the mass production of his 'light bulb'. They are used in most of our home luminaires and will remain the standard socket despite the decision to phase incandescent lamps out.

Newer light sources have had to develop a different fixing method as they differ from incandescent lamps radically in size and shape. Most halogen, fluorescent and metal halide lamps require bi-pin sockets. The bi-pin sockets have to accept only two metal pins. Depending on the lamp shape they are either simply pushed into the connector or are turned into their sockets.

The two pins on each side of the tubular fluorescent lamp, for example, are turned into the sockets. For some time, this was the sole shape and therefore fixing method for a fluorescent light source, until new U- or O-shaped fluorescents demanded a new way of fixing and therefore a new connector type. The development of the compact fluorescent lamp, on the other hand, seeks to adapt the size and shape of the lamp in order to fit into existing widespread E27 and E14 sockets.

This is all driven by a market for longer-lasting and more efficient alternatives to incandescent lamps. The same development can be observed in the new LED market. Either new LED connection methods emerge or the manufacturers enter the huge existing market by creating LED lights that fit into existing sockets.

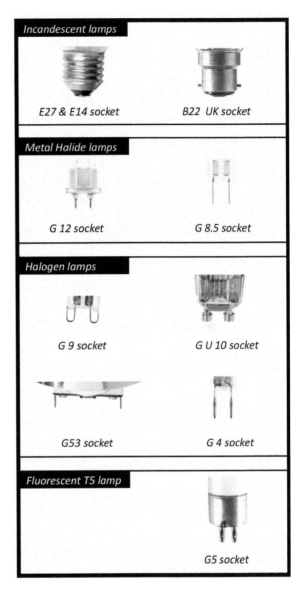

Fig. 1.19 Socket requirement for common lamp types.

LIGHT EMITTING DIODE – LED

There is a new kid on the block seeking to replace all existing luminaires and outperform them. LEDs are revolutionizing our industry and are clearly able to supersede existing lamp performance. Due to their compact dimensions, they create new possibilities in luminaire design and allow for greater creativity when designing with light. Before comparing the old versus

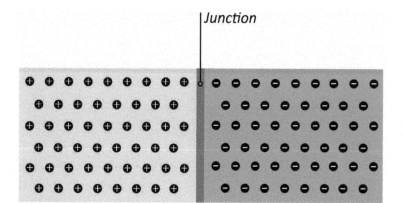

Junction

Positive   Negative

Fig. 1.20 Semi-conductive positive and negative layer separated by a junction.

the new, one should understand the basic principles of the Light Emitting Diode and its origins.

Function

Unlike the 'old' light sources, an LED is based on solid state technology. This means that no delicate filaments and gas are used. It makes the LED extremely robust against vibration and impacts. LEDs are based on diode technology. A diode consists of two semi-conductive materials. P is the positive region and N is negative region, and these are joined by a junction. When a current is applied, electricity can pass in one direction but not the other. Light is emitted when electrons pass the N region towards the P region where they fill the missing electron gaps. While doing so, the electrons fall into a lower energy state, lose energy and emit photons.

History

It took almost 100 years from the discovery of diodes emitting light to our modern LEDs, which are capable of generating white light. As with many inventions, it was an international joint venture where one discovery built on others. It all started in 1907 in the UK where H.J. Round reported light emission when experimenting with the first semi-conductor diodes. In 1962, more than half a century later, Nick Holonyak, 'the father of the light emitting diode', developed the first LED that generated visible light. These first LEDs emitted light in red only and were initially too expensive to be found in our daily lives. In the 1970s, mass production enabled the spread of seven-digit displays in watches and calculators. It wasn't until 1995 when Shuji Nakamura and his team developed the bright blue LED, which enabled them to create white light soon after. Shuji received the Nobel Prize for Physics for his discovery. Just as with the fluorescent lamp, the key to generating the right light lies in the second medium called phosphor. Everyone who is familiar with the addition of primary colour of light knows that red and blue light turn into yellow light. Mixing yellow with blue light creates white light. In an LED lamp, the blue light gets transformed into white light when passing through the yellow phosphor layer. The phosphor coating transforms part of the light into yellow light, allowing blue light to pass through unchanged at the same time. The blue and yellow light mix into white light. The thicker the phosphor layer, the more of the blue light gets transformed into yellow light. The light emitted by the LED then appears more yellow and warmer.

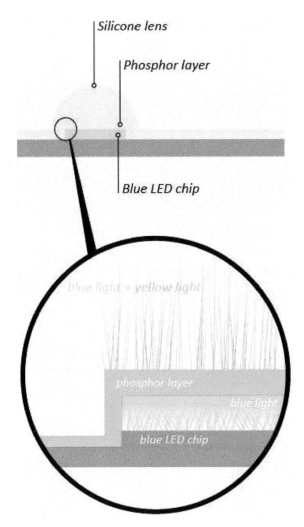

Silicone lens

Phosphor layer

Blue LED chip

blue light + yellow light

phosphor layer

blue light

blue LED chip

Fig. 1.21 Phosphor layer transforms blue LED light into white light.

Production: binning and MacAdam

LED-chip production is not very different from computer-chip production. It takes place in dust-free rooms where micro-millimetre-thin layers are applied on top of each other. Despite the clean room environment and the precise technology, controlling the production process is still very difficult. Impurities and variation do still apply and lead to differences in the colour temperature and brightness of LEDs. Therefore, all LEDs are tested separately and binned (a process of sorting by performance and the colour of light produced). Some manufacturers do

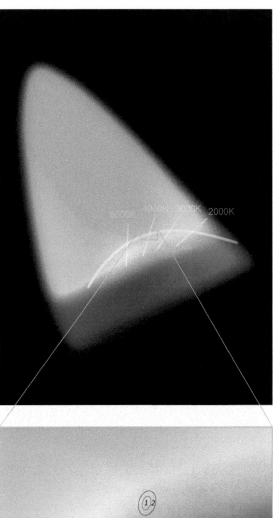

Fig. 1.22 CIE chart.

this more accurately than others. The human eye is very sensitive and able to notice even the smallest differences in colour. Not accurately binned LED lamps in the same room will emit light in different colour temperatures. Our eye picks it up and we perceive it as abnormality.

To help us to define the quality of LED light we use MacAdam's research. He tested the sensitivity of the human eye to light colour. His tests define a small oval area within the CIE colour space diagram.

LED-emitted white light within this oval cannot be distinguished by the human eye. This indicates one MacAdam step accuracy. Two MacAdam steps define a bigger oval. Few people looking at an LED light source binned under the two-step oval are able to see the difference of the white. Good LED manufacturers bin within two MacAdam steps. The bigger the MacAdam step number the more likely it is that you will see a colour variance between two LEDs. Binning has is price if one wants to guarantee the quality of LEDs. There are other means of making sure that the white light emission throughout a production range is constant, whether it is by combining many LEDs to get one specific colour temperature or working on the phosphor coating. What essentially counts is the guarantee of a manufacturer to offer a consistent white where a deviation from one lamp to the other is as small as possible and not noticeable.

Keep it cool

If an LED was able to choose its ideal place in the world to function it would probably prefer the two polar regions. Unlike incandescent lamps, LEDs have to be kept cool otherwise the heat-sensitive diode gets destroyed. Therefore, an important factor in ensuring that LEDs last a long time is thermal management. The level of thermal management depends on the electric current and the voltage applied to an LED. Modern LED are designed to run efficiently but there is a desire to get more and more light out of them. This means usually a higher current creating thermal stress on the LED. In a standard linear LED profile this is usually not a problem. Many small LEDs create a lot of light in a line. The aluminium profile they are mounted on has a large enough surface area to deflect the produced heat.

It gets problematic when the LEDs generate a lot of light on a small surface. Here a special heat

Fig. 1.23 Passive heatsink. (Cool Innovations)

sink is required to deal with the excessive amount of heat. The metal heat sink must be mounted to the back of the LED and usually carries a lot of fins. This increases its surface area and allows for a good heat exchange. These heat sinks are also called passive heat sinks.

Once installed in a fixture, the LED and its heat sink need enough space and air to avoid heat accumulation and to guarantee a carefree function. Space is often an issue when designing with light and every millimetre can be precious. Active cooling offers a solution and reduces the heat-sink size significantly while allowing one to drive the LED very high. A fan makes sure that air passes quickly along the cooling fins, speeding up the cooling process.

Fig. 1.24 Active fan-heatsink.
(Cool Innovations)

One should, however, consider that it is yet another component. The noise level must be controlled, it has a lifetime of its own and additional costs.

LED lamp types

Its size makes the LED extremely flexible and allows it to be shaped in any form needed. Some LED modules have become standard throughout the years. Most lighting manufacturers use these modules in their luminaires in one form or another.

The most common one available in high-street specialist stores is LED tape.

Originally designed to be glued into a profile, it is unfortunately found everywhere bare. It is glued and rolls out throughout our homes on top of and under cabinets, into coffers, wardrobes and any other place big enough for it. Many tapes are not fit for purpose. Exposed circuitry, LEDs and cables leave the product open to contact, dust and water, decreasing its life expectancy. The manufacturer might guarantee a long life but this clearly applies to ideal conditions only. Construction sites are dusty and dirty, and tapes and cables often get buckled. A lighting designer specifying tapes as luminaires will not be able to guarantee that the product will function as promised. LED tape manufacturers won't give you a guarantee if parts of the LED tape fail so the blame falls on the specifier. LED tapes should only be specified with an extrusion casing or in protected and covered joinery details. The same applies to the rigid LED strips.

Unlike tape, they need either physical mounting or an aluminium profile holding them into position. The cutting increments on flexible and solid strips vary. Rigid LED strips where the circuit mounting board consists of metal can often be run under

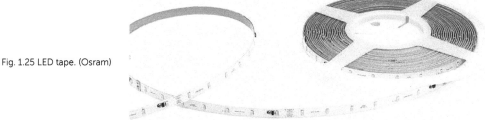

Fig. 1.25 LED tape. (Osram)

Fig. 1.26 Rigid LED strip. (KKDC)

Fig. 1.27 Single LED mounted onto an aluminium board. (Osram)

higher intensity than LED tapes. Most of the dimensions are standardized. The ability to run rigid strips brighter and their solid nature make them an ideal element to be used in linear extrusion profiles of all kinds.

The single high-output LED chip is often mounted to a board that is designed to allow an easy fixing into a future luminaire.

The mounting board acts as a first cooling plate and provides a bigger surface if cooling is required. In most environments, the simple 1w chip will not need cooling unlike 3w chips or higher. As almost all LEDs spread light in a 120-degree beam angle, a lens is required to change the beam angle as needed. A plastic lens covers the single lens, creating the desired beam angle. However, the light output of a 1w or 3w LED is often not enough if one wants to

create the same amount of light as in a downlight luminaire. New boards in all shapes with three or more high-output LEDs guarantee that the light output will be sufficient and lenses can be mounted. A multi array board allows the usage of extremely narrow beam lenses, keeping the overall size of the lamp, including the heat sink, compact.

LED modules are mounted on a puck-sized module and can produce the same output as multi array LEDs but do require a reflector that builds up, making the luminaire bigger. They are built on a modular base allowing them to be replaced easier if another output is required. A single light source is perceived by many as more pleasing than a dotted array of lights.

Not designed to create a pool of lights but a more diffused light are the bigger LED boards.

Ideal for lit panels, they have an even array of LEDs spread over a bigger board. When put behind an opal diffuser sheet at a certain distance they create an even diffused light. Some manufacturers offer the option of mixing warm white with cold white, putting the two different LED chips beside each other. For the club environment there are panels available with RGB (Red, Green, Blue) LEDs. They are designed

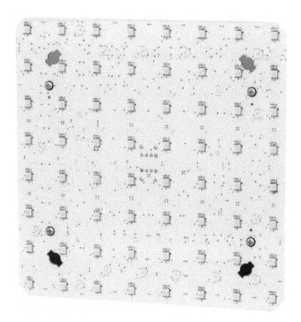

Fig. 1.28 Cluster of LEDs mounted onto a circuit board. (Traxon)

Fig. 1.29 Retro-fit LED lamps. (Osram)

to generate various colours, altering in a time loop if necessary.

The retro fits

All LED types previously mentioned have nothing to do with the traditional lamp market and its standardized light sockets. Everybody seems to be doing his or her own board and heat sink. This makes LED replacement by a third party impossible and it covers only a small part of the market.

One has to bear in mind that the conventional light sources with their sockets have been used for many years. Their design for quick replacement makes them and the retro fixtures so attractive. Most of the market still runs on the tradition lamp socket types. This is where the retro-fit lamps come into play. The first wave of retro fits came with compact fluorescent lamps. Now LED retro-fit lamps are dominating the market, serving almost all traditional lamp sockets. One can find LED lamps screwing into E27 sockets or fitting into GU 5.3 bi-pin sockets.

It is important to be able to compare the previous with the new. In order to understand whether the new LED is a match for the old, one has to take into consideration all the factors previously mentioned. What is the life expectancy? What colour temperature does it generate? What are its colour renditions and lumen output? What is the colour consistency of the replacement lamp? Most of the data is printed on the side of the lamp package, allowing us to compare different products.

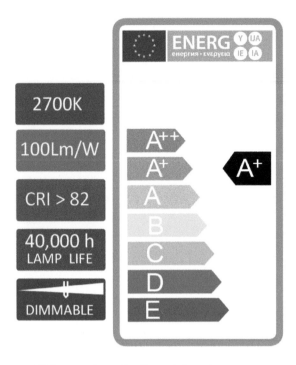

Fig. 1.30 Example of retro-fit LED lamp information.

The high price of LEDs used to put most people off, but prices are dropping and more people are now buying LEDs. Some of the big lamp manufacturers have already stopped producing traditional lamps and are only offering LED lamps. Their performance does in many cases match the traditional lamp types especially when it comes to efficiency but exceeds all lamps when it comes to lifetime expectancy. Still, one can see in many supermarkets, that retro fixtures are advancing and are marginalizing previous light sources. Price and dimmability keep the remaining incandescent lamps on the shelf but this is due to change soon, as LED luminaires become more and more sophisticated. LEDs are mimicking the beautiful performance of an incandescent lamp not only in their perfect colour rendition and the warm light they emit but also in their behaviour when dimmed. A dimmed incandescent light source emits warmer light the more it is dimmed. Modern LEDs and their drivers are able to imitate this warm dimming behaviour, making them ever

more attractive for the domestic market and the residential lighting scheme.

All lighting designers have switched completely to LEDs either driven by the requirements of the client to hit energy efficiency targets or because they believe that this will give the client a sustainable scheme. The aim is to provide the client with a lighting scheme that is as efficient as it is future-proof. In this case, we should guarantee that the LEDs and their specified drivers are exchangeable. A scheme is not future-proof if one must exchange the entire fitting rather than just a component.

LED life cycle

When the first LEDs entered the market, their lifetime was stated as being 50,000 hours or more. This is, of course, a huge improvement when compared with a fluorescent lamp lasting 20,000 hours and the life cycle of metal halide lamps with 15,000 hours. Soon it became evident that the first LEDs on the market started to fail sooner than expected. Every system is only as good as its weakest component. An LED lamp has many components. To make the matter worse, many sensitive electronic components are driven on the edge of the possible. A system that is not well designed will inevitably fail where it has been neglected most. Heat management was and is one of the main reasons for the premature failure of LEDs. The overheating of the LED is often due to badly designed heat sinks or a poor glue bond with the heat sink. The driver is the second key factor within an LED system. LEDs are very sensitive when exposed to higher currents and current spikes. A good driver will supply the LED with the exact current needed and control circuit spikes. With good heat management, a good LED board design and the right current supply an LED can run for a long time. It will not stop working outright but decrease its light output and become less efficient over time. The driver tends to have a shorter life cycle and will in this case fail prior to the LED.

Environmental acceptability of LED lamps

A replacement LED lamp is effectively an electronic component and can be disposed of as such. While metal halide and incandescent lamps consist only of glass and metal components, each LED replacement lamp caries the integral diver within it. There are no really harmful materials in an LED lamp, but recycling programs are already in place, taking advantage of the valuable material within each replacement lamp.

Flexible and rigid LED strips generally operate in the same way. Most of the linear LEDs are fully glued and integrated with the driver into luminaires. Should one component fail the entire fixture needs to be disposed of. Some conscious luminaire manufacturers using linear LED boards are changing their approach, however, and are allowing for the replacement of the various individual components when they fail.

Dimmability of LEDs

In theory, all LEDs are dimmable. The amount of electric current passing through an LED determines how bright it will shine. Therefore, the driver determines whether an LED dims or not. Retro-fit LED lamps have an integral driver which in many cases does not allow dimming. This applies to most of the retro-fit lamps available on our high streets. High-end retro-fit LEDs, however, usually do allow dimming and are therefore more expensive.

The LEDs without integral drivers are dependent on external drivers when it comes to dimming. In fact, the driver plays a key role here. A good-quality driver tested with the LED boards used will allow a smooth dimming down to zero per cent without flickering and jumps. When specifying LEDs in a project it is often essential to double-check what driver is used and how the dimming behaviour is. An LED is only as good as the driver running it, especially when it comes to interlinking it with a complex LED control system.

RGB and dynamic LEDs

With the introduction of the missing blue LED at the end of the 1990s the first white light was created by simply putting a red, green and blue LED beside each other. When moving away from the three-coloured light dots, the eye merges the three-light point making it appear white.

This method makes use of the additive colour mixing of light when perceived from far away. What's more important is that literally all colours can be

Fig. 1.31 Close-up of an RGB LED video display.

created this way. However, the observer will always have to stand at a certain distance from the LED to not see the singlelight colour dots.

Many of these red, green and blue light colour dots can generate graphic or moving images. We all know this method on a big scale where it finds its use in giant LED screens at rock concerts or in display boards on buildings. The content shown is bright and sharp and allows the display of moving images, graphics, animation and text. The distance-visibility ratio depends on the LED pitch. This is the distance of one RGB LED to the next. The smaller the pitch, the closer a non-pixelated image can be created by the human eye. In an architectural context, the high-resolution LED screen is not often used as in many cases the content distracts from the architecture. RGB LEDs can be placed with a wider pitch when diffused behind opal glass or acrylic. The

diffuser transforms the LED screen into a mood wall, allowing it to create abstract moving paintings on a wall. When content, dimensions and position are used sensitively it can support the architecture immensely.

RGB LEDs are used in many applications today from the giant LED screen, a thin linear diffused LED strip or super-strong projectors dyeing skyscrapers into changing colours. The three separate LEDs are rare these days; they are generally replaced by an LED generating red, green and blue light within a single chip. The colour it mixes is of excellent quality but it will certainly fail to produce a good white light. White light from an RGB LED has the tendency to drift towards one colour. It can be perceived as pinkish, turquoise or greenish. Therefore, if white is needed in good quality, one should use a pure white rather than trying

Fig. 1.32 Wide 30mm (1.4in) pitch RGB LED board behind etched glass. The glass prevents pixilation of the LED from creating a blurred image. (Arch: Carbondale; Lights: Mindseye; Photo: Andy Spain)

Figure 1.33 Dynamic white LED spotlight. The separate warm white and cold white LEDs can be mixed to create the desired white.

to reproduce it with an RGB LED. White can be mixed as well. There are so-called dynamic white LEDs mixing warm and cold white light in a single chip. This allows one to change the colour of the white light emitted. These LEDs are used in many different places. Dynamic white luminaires are used in home, office and shop lighting schemes. The white can be changed from a cold bright midday light to a warm welcoming evening light. Both RGB and dynamic white LEDs are able to change the feeling of a space through a change in colour and movement.

White and RGB LEDs used in combination can be an ideal solution, as this not only allows one to create a good white but also a saturated colour if needed. This is achieved by using an RGB and a white LED product beside each other, controlling each as needed and mixing them to achieve the desired effect. This is obviously a complicated process demanding a lot of adjustment work not only in laying out but also in control. This is why some manufacturers are starting to produce white and coloured RGB light within a single chip or on a same board. This allows one to create an extremely versatile light. When mixed

Figure 1.34 Multicolour LEDs and white LEDs in a single LED strip tape. These can either be used separately or mixed. (Osram)

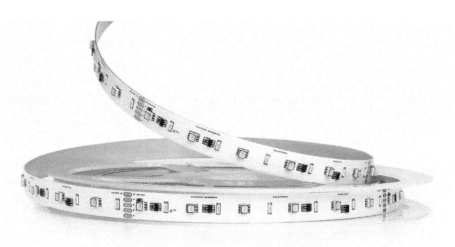

together, these LEDs can generate pastel light tones. More importantly, light can be tuned for the desired application.

A fixture fitted with a white RGB LED can produce a reddish white for the meat counter, a cold blue white for the fishmonger or a warm white for the baker, all with a single light fixture and no need to exchange the light source.

Whilst traditional lamps are in decline, the LED as a light source is rising. It is only a matter of time until it replaces the existing lamps completely. There are many LED lamps on the market capable of matching and exceeding the properties of their predecessors. It is up to the lighting designer to choose whether the LED is to be used or the old lamp is to be given another last chance. The decision will depend on the comparative price of the products in relation to the performance needed. Eventually, conventional light sources will survive only in a few niche markets, before being eclipsed entirely.

Chapter 2

LUMINAIRES

FUNCTION, COMPONENTS AND TYPES

N OW THAT WE HAVE A FULL UNDERSTAND-
ing of the various lamp types it is time to
take a look at how the lamps are used. To
be able to run a lamp safely one needs a light fixture,
which is also called a luminaire.

A light fixture usually consists of a lamp, lamp
holder, and a cable providing the socket and lamp
with power. Often a casing is necessary to protect
either the user from the electricity within the luminaire or to protect the light fixture from external
influences. In many cases, a transformer, also called a
driver or ballast, is necessary to provide the lamp with
the right power. To guide the light, many luminaires
use shades, reflectors and lenses.

The above is the rule although some designers like
to play with the arrangement of the various components.

Figure 2.01 Components of a luminaire.

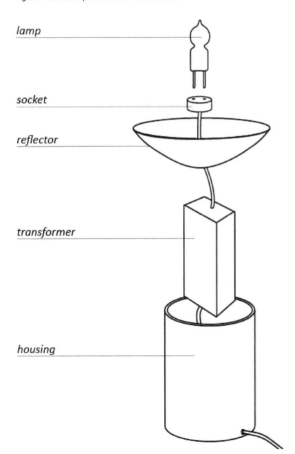

lamp

socket

reflector

transformer

housing

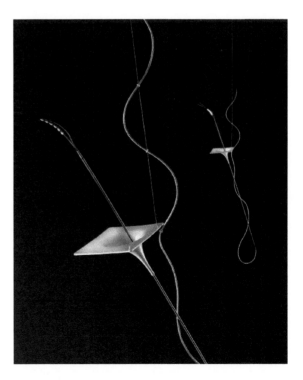

Figure 2.02 A luminaire where the light source can withdraw into
the reflector.

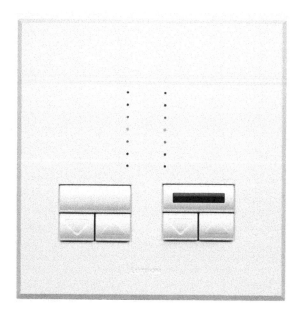

Figure 2.03 Wall-mounted dimmer. (Lutron)

DIMMERS, TRANSFORMERS, DRIVERS AND BALLASTS

Dimmers

Luminaires that are designed to work with incandescent lamps or 240-volt halogen lamps do not require transformers and are simple in design. This keeps the light fitting fail-safe. When they fail, it is usually only the lamp that needs replacement. They can all be dimmed with a conventional dimmer.

A dimmer restricts the current that the lamp gets. It simply cuts the alternating current supply to the lamp, leaving the lamp with less power. The simplest and most commonly used dimming method is leading-edge dimming. Leading-edge dimming cuts off the front of each incoming alternating current. Most common household dimmer switches are leading-edge dimmers.

Transforming electricity

The various sockets that each lamp requires have been mentioned in the previous chapter. Each socket is designed to hold the lamp but also to supply it with power. The lamp shape and the electrical requirements dictate the design and the material of a socket. The power that is needed by a lamp is not always equal to the power that is provided by the grid. The standard power outlet in our buildings ranges from 110v–240v. An electric transformer is necessary to supply the power the lamp requires. When working with luminaires one soon stumbles over three main elements when it come to devices transforming electricity. There is the ballast, the transformer and the driver. They all do the same thing, changing the mains electricity to a different value, yet they work differently.

Ballasts

Electrical ballasts are necessary to run fluorescent, neon and compact fluorescent lamps. They provide the initial high voltage to start the fluorescent lamp and then restrict the current that a lamp receives to avoid damage to the lamp. Ballasts do so with resistors, magnets and inductors while the electronic ballast achieves the same with its integral circuit

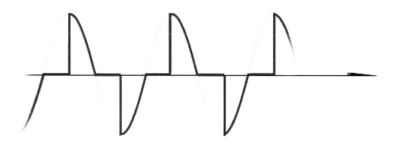

Figure 2.04 Leading-edge dimming principle.

Figure 2.05 Ballast for fluorescent T5 lamps.
(Lutron)

board. Electronic ballasts have mostly replaced traditional ballasts as they are more efficient and guarantee flicker-free dimming at a frequency of 20,000hz. Not all lamps are dimmable but with the introduction of the electronic ballast, fluorescent lamps became dimmable. One must be careful, however, when dimming a florescent lamp too low as one might experience an unwanted colour shift. The same applies to exposing fluorescent lamps to a colder environment. Special ballasts are required to fire fluorescents up and keep them running in lower temperatures.

Transformers

Power transformers are used to transfer a high primary mains current to a lower secondary current. To effectively run low-voltage halogen lamps, the voltage has to be dropped to 12v or 24v. An analogue transformer achieves this with one magnetic coil and two separate windings. The primary winding delivers 240v to the coil. The steel core acts as a transfer magnet and transfers electricity to the second coil with fewer windings.

This results in a lower voltage output of 12v or 24v with alternating frequency. This analogue principle makes sure that you get a transformer that is long-lasting but also more expensive, bigger, heavier and less efficient than a so-called electronic transformer.

Electronic transformers are not fully electronic and work largely on the same principle as their big analogue brothers, with one essential difference: a much smaller core allowing the transformer size to shrink significantly. In order for this to happen, it changes our 240v standard mains alternating frequency current of 50hz or 60hz to a much higher frequency and into a direct current. The small core transforms the 240v into 12v, 24v or other voltages. Dimmable low-voltage transformers are widely available.

If one wants an electronic transformer to perform well and avoid buzzing when dimmed, one has to make sure that the incoming current arrives from the appropriate type of dimmer, for example, a

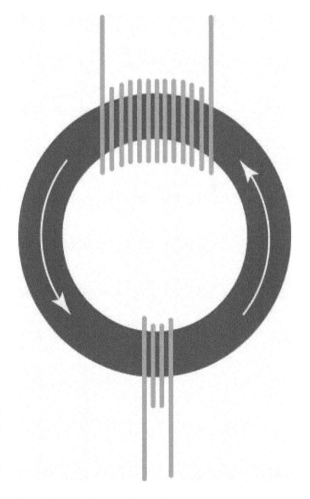

Figure 2.06 Principle of a coil transformer.

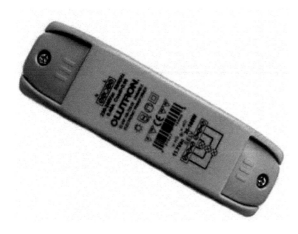

Figure 2.07 Example of an electronic trailing-edge transformer. (Lutron).

trailing-edge dimmer. Let's remember that a conventional domestic dimmer usually sits within the wall switch box and regulates the current reaching the transformer. The trailing-edge dimmer cuts off the end of each incoming alternating current – when it reaches its highest point it cut off and goes directly to zero.

Drivers

A transformer providing the right current or voltage for an LED is called an LED driver. They function on the same principle as low-voltage transformers. However, they are designed to run on a much smaller

Figure 2.08 Trailing-edge dimming principle.

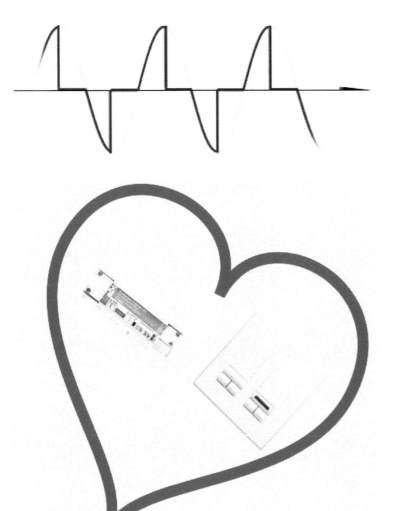

Figure 2.09 Relationship between the electronic transformer and trailing-edge dimmer.

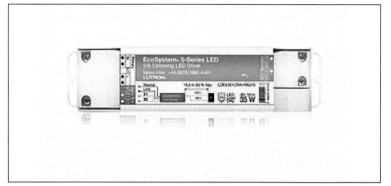

Figure 2.10 LED driver (Lutron).

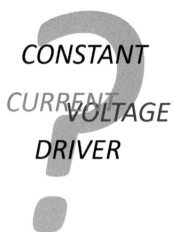

CONSTANT

CURRENT VOLTAGE

DRIVER

Figure 2.11 Constant current or constant voltage driver?

electric load than transformers. They are optimized to provide the LED with the right power.

The current consumption of an LED has to be controlled tightly. The performance of an LED varies with the driving current. If an LED doesn't receive enough current, it will not shine bright enough, while if too high a current is provided it will shine brighter. Brighter does sound better but if the heat management of an LED is not designed for the driving current it will decrease its life span or lead to a premature failure of the LED.

Constant current drivers offer a good solution as they are designed to keep the current stable, making sure the LED performs well and dims appropriately. This driver type is ideal if one wants to runs a single high-performance LED from one driver. If, however, many different LEDs are run on a single constant current driver, the voltage within an electronic circuit may vary, which will lead to varying performances.

The solution is a so-called constant voltage driver. They make sure that the voltage doesn't change regardless of the LED types used. They are preferred when one has to drive various LED strips in parallel and series. This is possible since many LED strips have onboard current regulators keeping the current constant. This method is not as efficient as the constant current method but when it comes to cabling, installation and driver quantities it is certainly the better choice.

SHADES, REFLECTORS, LENSES AND DIFFUSERS

Shades

The three traditional primary functions of shades are still important today. With the introduction of bright electric light came the need to soften it. Edison's light bulb was often perceived as too strong compared to the previous gloomy gas lights. As well as softening the light, shades also cover lamps and decorate the room. Shades come in all shapes, sizes, colours and materials. They define the quality and amount of the light emitted.

Figure 2.12 Lampshade, Lampampe by Ingo Mauer.

Reflectors

Deliberate reflection of light can be traced back further than the invention of the electrical light. Light from candles and fire in lighthouses was redirected by mirrors and reflective metals. These reflectors had the aim of increasing the efficiency of the light, focusing all the available light into a desired direction. Not much has changed since then. Reflectors in today's luminaires still redirect light, mostly with the help of formed reflective metal sheets. The efficiency, however, has improved since than. Whether for diffused fluorescent lamps and linear LEDS or point sources like halogen lamps and LED engines – today's reflectors are often designed with the help of computers, making sure that the light created performs exactly as expected. They are chosen according to the function and amount of light needed from the luminaire.

Reflector finish

With the finish of the aluminium reflector (whether polished, textured, matte or white), one is able to influence the quality of light.

A polished reflector is highly effective and will create a crisp light beam, with the edges of the light beam finish instantly creating a defined image of light on the illuminated surface. However, as the highly reflective surface mirrors the light source, it can cause glare when looked at from an undesired angle.

Polished textured reflectors soften the light. One will get a more diffused light spot on the ground. The level of diffusion can be controlled by the type of texture. Matte or white reflectors are less effective but they do create a soft light. The matte and white surface reflectors are more pleasing to the eye. They reflect the light using matte surfaces,

Figure 2.13 Polished, textured and matte reflector finishes.

which reduces glare when looking at them. This makes them the preferred choice of architects and designers even though they are less effective than a polished reflector.

Reflector shape and direction

The majority of reflectors are made from bent or pressed aluminium sheets. The shape of the reflector and its position defines how the light is emitted – whether it leaves the luminaire though a narrow or wide opening and whether it shines directly downwards or at an angle. Reflectors for fluorescent T5 lamps are divided into narrow, medium, wide and asymmetric reflectors.

Light from point sources can be directed more precisely than the light of diffused fluorescent tubes. Their reflectors can create a light beam that is defined by its beam angle. The beam angle generally ranges from a narrow five-degree to the so-called flood sixty-degree beam angle.

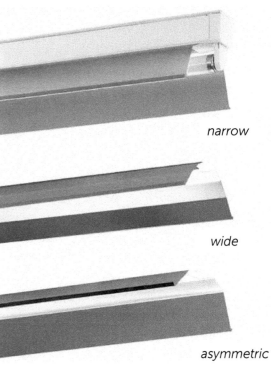

narrow

wide

asymmetric

Figure 2.14 Fluorescent T5 batten with various reflectors.

Figure 2.15 Interchangeable reflector. (Reggiani)

Figure 2.16 Tight and intense 8-degree beam spot to a softer 48-degree flood spot. (iGuzzini)

A tight beam angle not only focuses the actual light beam but also allows it to 'transport' the light further than a wide beam angle with the same light source. A tight beam angle creates an intense light spot suitable for accentuating an object while wide beam angles are more suited to covering surfaces and general areas. Beside the various beam angles, one has the choice of asymmetric reflectors. They are usually designed to throw light at an angle covering the perpendicular surface.

Lenses

Lenses were used long before the introduction of LED lamps. But they are a new factor to be considered within luminaires since the progress of LED. The cold LED light source has allowed cheap and easy-to-manufacture plastic lenses to develop. Just like reflectors, they deform the beam shape of the light emitted by the LED. Most LED strips and 1w or 3w LEDs emit light in a 120-degree beam. LED lenses are attached directly to the LED and generate either a tighter or a wider beam angle.

Figure 2.17 Bespoke LED tube using recessed light from the shelf lenses. (Mindseye Lighting)

Figure 2.18 The external bespoke lens is part of the design language. (Erco)

There are many LED lens manufacturers offering a wide range of lenses that can be mounted directly onto the LED board.

This allows a luminaire manufacturer to design a luminaire using LED boards and lenses almost like a Lego set. If a luminaire contains more than one LED, each light beam of the LED can be controlled separately.

Many luminaire manufacturers choose to design and produce their own lenses, which enables them to control quality and tailor the light to their needs.

Lenses create little glare and are very versatile. From lenses creating extremely narrow beam angles, lenses generating oval beams to side-emitting lenses, almost anything is possible.

Lenses can also be found in many retro-fit LED light sources. Most of them change the directional 120-degree beam into a multidirectional 360-degree beam angle.

Diffusers

Unlike the reflector, which concentrates light, a diffuser spreads it. Whether made out of etched glass or plastic their function is to hide the light source and to soften the light. When used in front of a reflector they soften the edges of a light and spread it more widely. Diffusers can be separated into: opal diffusers, satin diffusers and micro prism diffusers.

Opal diffusers

Opal diffusers are plain white and reflective. Traditional opal diffusers are made of white opal glass and are primarily used when high diffusion is necessary and a lamp image is not wanted. The light source is not visible but creates a uniformly lit white opal surface. The lamp can be placed closer to the diffuser, allowing the fitting to be more compact. This high diffusion, however, comes at a price – it will make the luminaire less efficient. Plastic diffusers mimic the opal diffuser and have replaced opal glass in most cases.

Figure 2.19 Opal diffuser. (BWF)

Figure 2.20 Luminaire with opal diffuser. (RZB Leuchten)

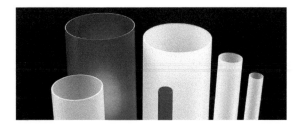

Figure 2.21 Satin diffuser. (BWF)

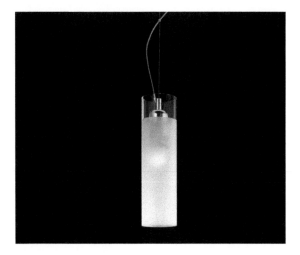

Figure 2.22 Luminaire with a satin diffuser. (Artemide)

Figure 2.23 Stretched ceiling. (BMW, Paris)

Satin diffusers

Satin diffusers look similar to etched or sandblasted glass. They come in different grades, transmitting either more light while diffusing less or vice versa. The more light is transmitted the more visible the lamp behind the diffuser sheet is. One can counter the visibility of the lamp by moving the light source further away from the diffuser. This might be more efficient but it also increases the depth of a luminaire.

Stretched membrane diffusers

Some bespoke fixtures use a stretched PVC membrane, also known as Barrisol or stretched ceiling, as a kind of light diffuser. PVC membranes come in rolls and are used with big luminaires and when the standardized diffuser sheet is too small.

Micro prism diffusers

Small micro prism diffusers, much like large stretch membrane diffusers, are not classic diffusers but are designed to achieve the same result. They diffuse light and mask the lamp image, controlling glare at the same time. Unlike the other diffusers, a micro prism diffuser is a transparent sheet containing many very small prisms. This makes it highly efficient but at the cost of lamp visibility. Micro prism is not able to disguise a lamp fully. The shape and size of the micro prism defines the level of diffusion. Many micro prisms are designed to diffuse the light while some are designed to redirect and control the light.

When they do the latter, they are called spreader lenses. The shape of the prisms changes a specific light

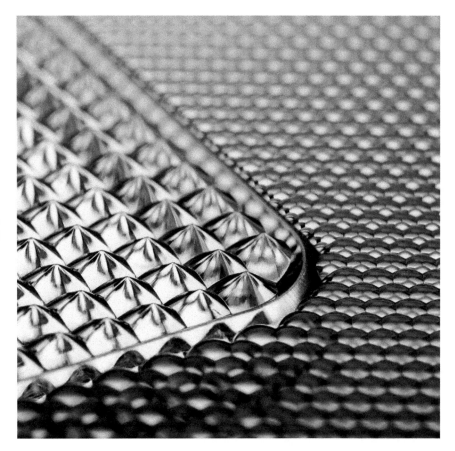

Figure 2.24 Micro prism. (Lumenwerx)

beam into another desired beam angle. Most common spreader lenses are so-called linear or oval spreader lenses. They change the round light projection of a lamp into an oval light shape. The light beam gets stretched into one direction only, allowing one to cover more area with a single light.

Spreader lenses are useful when lighting artwork on walls or to reduce the number of luminaires used in a corridor. The other type of spreader lens diffuses, softens and enlarges the light beam evenly. All spreader lenses rely on a reflector creating a defined light beam.

Not only is the actual beam angle changeable but also the colour of a lamp. There is a range of colour filters available, allowing us to change white light into a red or blue light colour. More importantly, filters allow us to colour-correct the white light of a lamp – for example, warm white light into a cold white light. An infrared filter removes all infrared light, making sure that no damaging light reaches light-sensitive art-work.

Both spreader lenses and filters give one the flexibility to change the light – optimizing and fine-tuning a lighting scheme while on site.

Filters change the light effect, keeping the light source visible. A louvre, on the other hand, is an

Figure 2.25 Linear spreader lens – magnet connection. (Soraa)

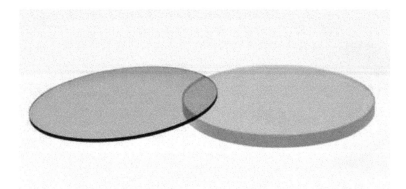

Figure 2.26 Light colour correction filter. (Leefilters)

Figure 2.27 Louvre attached directly to the lamp. (Soraa)

accessory designed to prevent one from seeing the light source to avoid unwanted glare. The louvre sits in front of the light source and will reveal the lamp only when looking almost directly into it. They can be integral to the luminaire or an external accessory.

Snoots or glare guards have a similar function in architectural lighting but achieve their goal differently. They are used in luminaires with a tight beam angle and are usually long cylindrical tubes added to a light fitting. They prevent one from seeing the light source more effectively than louvres. Snoots are applied in fixtures that are angled towards passers-by, often at a critical angle. In all cases, restricting glare is the primary function. Snoots can also limit light spill and define a light spot by creating sharp edges.

Some snoots have integral light shapers, allowing the ultimate control over the light exiting luminaires. The beam can be shaped by movable metal fins called framers. This allows one, for example, to change a round light spot into a square or rectangular light.

Externally applied, they are called barn doors and are mostly used when illuminating artwork, sculptures and where a precise control of light is necessary.

Figure 2.28 Spotlight without snoot, glare guard and long snoot. (Precision Lighting)

Figure 2.29 Projector track light with internal 'framers'. (iGuzzini)

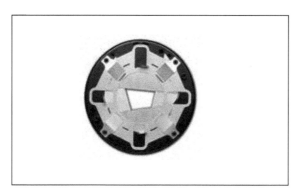

Figure 2.30 Track light with internal 'framers'. (iGuzzini)

Figure 2.31 Barn doors. (iGuzzini)

Gobos can help to create a special atmosphere within a space. They are metal or glass templates and sit in front of the lamp off a projector luminaire, allowing the projection of images and pattern onto a surface.

Figure 2.32 Projector track light using a gobo projector. (iGuzzini)

Figure 2.33 Gobo template for a projector. (iGuzzini)

LUMINAIRE TYPES

Luminaire types are usually separated by function and position.

There are free-standing luminaires and table-top luminaires that are movable and can add light to an existing lighting scheme. Non-movable luminaires are ceiling, wall and floor fixtures that are mounted to their support. These types can be further separated into recessed, surface-mounted and suspended luminaires.

Decorative luminaires (all about the look]

The design and light created by the aforementioned types of luminaire separates the luminaires further into decorative and technical or architectural

Figure 2.34 If, on a project, one gets stuck trying to find a light solution for a particular area, simply stepping back and reminding oneself of the main luminaire types can help.

luminaires. Decorative luminaires are light sources where the main emphasis is on the appearance and style of the luminaire. The design or the style of the light can be an eye-catcher and visually dominate a room or allow the luminaire to fit visually into an interior design scheme. Surface-mounted luminaires, pendants and free-standing lights are in many cases part of this category. The styles vary from Georgian and country all the way to retro and contemporary. Decorative light sources are an essential part of an interior design scheme and will often be selected by either the interior designer or architect. Good lighting designers have an excellent knowledge of the luminaires available on the market and often assist in sourcing luminaires. Most lighting design consultancies have a luminaire library, part of which is dedicated to decorative lighting. Lighting fairs and frequent visits from luminaire manufacturers' representatives enable a lighting designer to stay up to date or ahead of their time.

Figure 2.35 CTO's Braque, a light adding accent yet merging nicely with the interior design. (Photo: Chris Everard)

Photo: Chris Everard

Figure 2.36 Ingo Maurer's *Zettl's*, a centrepiece in any room.

While the selection of decorative luminaires is in some cases optional, lighting designers must have a say when it comes to the positioning of the luminaire and its performance. The light effect and the feel that a decorative light emits is our main concern. A bedside light, for example, with a black or metal shade covering most of the necessary light might not be useful as a reading light.

Does the luminaire have exposed visible lamps and cause unpleasant glare? Is the light bright enough for reading and can it be adjusted if necessary? Most of these questions are best resolved by getting samples of the luminaires in and testing them.

Architectural luminaires (all about the light)

The other big category is architectural light fittings. They are mostly integral and surface-mounted; if not, they are certainly designed to be perceived as part of the architectural fabric of a building. Their primary function is to provide a space and the objects within that space with the light needed. Alongside this functional aspect, the visual and technical integration into the architecture is equally important. Luminaires for a warehouse or a metro station will have to differ from luminaires for a jewellery shop or conference centres. The conditions in these spaces and their requirements couldn't be more different.

Ceiling luminaires

Most luminaires are naturally positioned in the ceiling. This is not only because it is the most natural place for the light and one can expect less glare from the light sources but also because most of the technical services of a building are hidden behind the ceiling. The ceiling void lends itself ideally to running the required electricity to the luminaires, host drivers or the entire light fittings.

Pendant luminaires

A pendant luminaire does not need a large void in the ceiling. These luminaires usually host their drivers and reflectors within the fitting away from the ceiling void. Pendants are ideal when there is little or no ceiling void available but also to bring the light down to the level needed, which in many cases will save energy.

Pendant luminaires can be divided into: luminaires emitting light in all directions equally, up-light pendants, down-light pendants, and up- and down-light pendant luminaires.

Up- or indirect lighting pendants rely on the ceiling to bounce the light off and spread it into the space. They create a pleasant diffused light. The light quality and level vary and will depend very much on ceiling colour and the distance of the luminaire from the ceiling. Indirect pendants create ambient light by bouncing light off the ceiling, spreading it softly all over the space.

Down-light pendants, on the other hand, illuminate the desired area only. The reflector or diffuser creates either a diffused or focused area of light.

Figure 2.37 Lighting principles of a pendant – multidirectional, up-lighting, down-lighting and up- and down-lighting.

They are usually positioned directly where light is necessary. Pendants lighting downwards provide an efficient and bright light locally while keeping the ambience in relative darkness. By doing so, they create a more intimate feeling.

Both pendant types create a very different ambience when combined, however, into a single up- and down-light pendant, which creates the ideal light for an office. They generate high local light levels while illuminating surrounding surfaces. This reduces the light contrast within a space.

Many technical up- and down-light pendants can be split into two control circuits. This means that the up-light can be controlled separately from the down-light. It allows one to create varying light scenes with a single fitting.

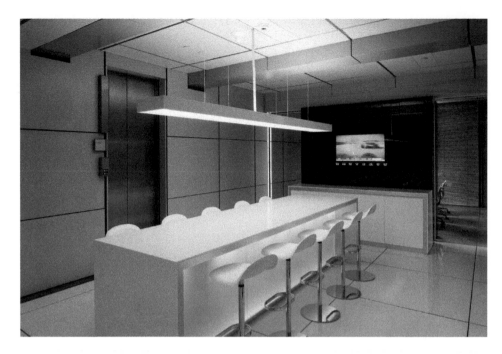

Figure 2.38
Bespoke pendant
with up- and
down-lights on
separate circuits.
(HSBC, Hong
Kong)

Ceiling surface-mounted luminaires

Surface-mounted luminaires are ideal when there is no ceiling void. Most suspended fixtures are available as surface-mounted versions, distributing light down and sidewards only. Whether they create a diffused or a directional light, ceiling-mounted luminaires are visible. Just as with pendants hanging in a space, the visual impact of ceiling-mounted lights has to be taken into consideration.

One can separate ceiling surface-mounted luminaires into diffused and directional luminaires.

The diffused luminaire types come in linear, square, round and other shapes. When arranged sensitively, following the architectural language of a space, they create little visual impact. They can, however, dominate the space and their impact can be spectacular when positioned in groups or against the architecture.

Directional luminaires form the other group of the ceiling surface luminaires. Track lights are a big part of this family. Although available as suspended types, the vast majority are ceiling-mounted. A track light consists of a track, adaptor and luminaire.

Figure 2.39 Diffused vs directed light.

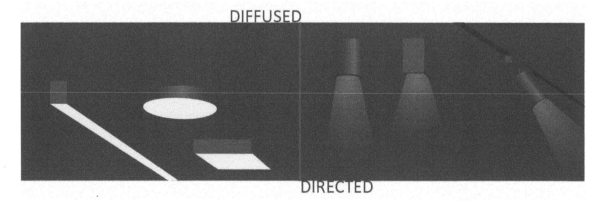

DIFFUSED

DIRECTED

Figure 2.40 Surface-mounted luminaires creating minimal visual impact (left) or maximal visual impact (right). Left, Hackney Marshes Community Centre, Stanton Williams Architects; Right: Rotunda Entrance, MAKE Architects.

Figure 2.41 Track-mounted luminaire. (Erco)

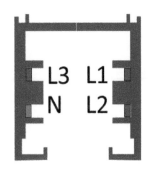

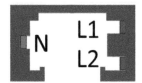

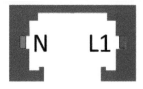

Figure 2.42 Three-, two- and one-circuit tracks.

3-circuit track   **2-circuit track**   **1-circuit track**

The track is the base of this luminaire type and can be recessed into the ceiling or surface-mounted. Although there are 12v versions available, most of the tracks are engineered to supply 120v, 230v and 277v. One can choose between one-, two- or three-circuit tracks. This means that, for example, a three-circuit track runs three different control circuits and that a luminaire attached to it can be assigned to any of the three circuits. Each circuit can be controlled separately. This means that on a single-track, fittings can be on and off at the same time, depending which circuit is activated.

The adaptor joins the fixture and the track and is attached to the luminaire. It enables one to quickly connect, remove and change the luminaires on the track. A switch on the adapter allows one to choose the circuit allocation. This manual circuit allocation is not necessary if the track comes with a data bus. The data bus permits the control of each luminaire separately and remotely.

On a track, all types of luminaire (spotlights, flood-lights and wallwashers) can be used and combined as desired. The fact that these elements are separately controllable makes this a highly flexible system. The track allows the lighting to change constantly to meet new requirements. Galleries, shops and multifunctional spaces profit most from this system solution.

Ceiling-recessed luminaires

Ceiling-recessed luminaires use the void within the ceiling to hide the light source. The biggest group of recessed luminaires are down-lights. The US-based company Kirling was one of the first manufacturers to develop recessed down-lights in the 1950s.

The recessed down-light, also known as the recessed can light, quickly evolved into the primary choice of illumination in new minimalist buildings following the 1950s. Disguised, it allows one to illuminate and enhance a space without dominating it.

The recess can hold various reflectors, making it a versatile lighting tool capable of realizing various light effects. Recessed down-lights might all look the same but their performance is determined by the reflector and lamp they conceal. There are three

Standard Downlight   Wall Washer   Adjustable Downlight

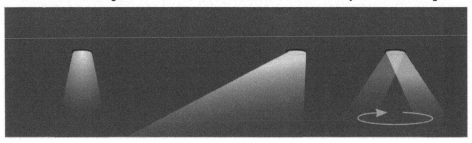

Figure 2.43 Three major point light sources – down-light types.

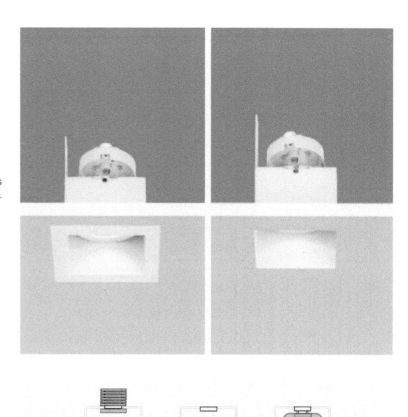

Figure 2.44 Bezel down-light and trimless down-light (Whitegoods).

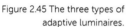

Figure 2.45 The three types of adaptive luminaires.

types of down-light with compact light sources: the standard down-light, the wallwasher and the adjustable down-light.

In its most simple form, it comes with a bezel that forms the frame holding the reflector and hiding the cut-out or aperture in the ceiling. The trimless finish is more sophisticated and comes without the bezel, reducing the visual impact of the fixture.

Depending on the reflector, it illuminates the space with a wide to very narrow light beam. Some manufacturers produce luminaires where the reflector can be exchanged. This enables the lighting to adapt in case the furniture layout or design of the space changes. There are three types of adaptive luminaire. The first type has a fixed LED or halogen lamp and allows one to change the beam spread by exchanging the reflector or lens. The second type has a standard lamp holder that takes lamps that come with a reflector. If one wants to change the beam angle, the lamp fixed to the reflector has to be replaced. The third option allows one to alter the beam angle by adding a refractor sheet or foil onto the reflector. A beam angle of fifteen degrees, for example, can be changed to twenty-four, thirty-six or sixty degrees with a simple action.

The wallwasher down-light forms a separate group. The position of the lamp and the design of the fixture differs here from standard down-lights. The light is reflected downwards at an angle and allows one, as the name says, to wash a wall with light evenly. To do so, the luminaires have to be a certain distance from the wall and from each other. The distance depends on the fixture type and room height.

The third and most flexible down-light group are the adjustable down-lights. The luminaire frame and

Figure 2.46 Wallwasher (Whitegoods). The distance of the luminaires from each other and to the wall must be right to achieve the optimal light distribution. The wallwasher's effect can be visualized in a lighting calculation.

light source are detached, which allows the light to be adjusted. The adjustable down-light doesn't differ greatly from the standard down-light – it is compact and has low visual impact. Its movement is often limited to one direction and to a small change in angle. Not so the gimbal down-light, as it allows for easy movement of the light beam in all directions.

This makes the light source more visible and it therefore has a higher visual impact. Both luminaire types are used when a lighting scheme requires limited or high flexibility.

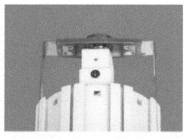

Figure 2.47 (Left) adjustable down-light and (right) gimbal down-light.

Linear ceiling-recessed luminaires

Most luminaire companies offer a range of linear luminaires, from suspended and surface-mounted to recessed linear luminaires. Recessed linear luminaires allow lighting to integrate into a space, reducing the visual impact yet delivering an even and pleasant diffused light. Recessed linears come in various standard sizes but can also be made to measure, allowing the lighting to follow the architecture exactly.

They come in various widths with different diffuser options. Some of them offer special wallwasher reflectors or lenses, making them ideal for washing a wall with light evenly without having to use multiple light sources.

Many lighting schemes require a diffused general light combined with areas accentuated by spotlights. Some linear luminaires offer a diffused linear light source combined with adjustable down-lights. This allows one to cover many lighting scenarios in one fitting yet avoiding visual clutter on the ceiling by reducing what is visible there.

Wall luminaires

Just as with ceiling luminaires there are surface-mounted and recessed wall luminaires. The wall-mounted luminaires are a popular alternative to ceiling luminaires when the ceiling cannot be touched. Many projects with intricate cornice details or concrete ceilings make the introduction of luminaires in the ceiling either undesirable or impossible. Or perhaps another type of light is not right

Figure 2.48 Recessed trimless linear used in a gallery.

Figure 2.49 Three major recessed linear luminaires types.

Wall Washer   Standard Linear   Linear & Downlight

for a space and a wall-mounted luminaire offers the desired light effect. We distinguish as with ceiling luminaires between surface-mounted and recessed luminaires. Both can be split into diffused and directional luminaires.

Diffused wall luminaires

Whether recessed or surface-mounted, diffused wall luminaires bring light down to our task level, spreading it evenly. Diffused light on walls is often found in

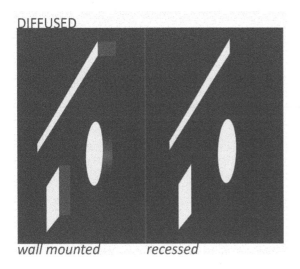

Figure 2.50 Diffused linear wall-mounted or recessed luminaires.

corridors and on staircases. The long luminaires can look very graphical and can give the space a direction.

Their visual impact is high. The selection of the right size and type to suit a space has to be done sensitively.

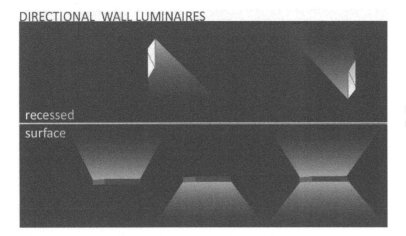

Figure 2.51 Directional luminaires can be recessed or surface-mounted.

Their light covers all the surfaces in a space evenly with little energy consumption.

Smaller diffused light sources also called marker lights can act as a single dot on the wall indicating an entrance or a change in direction in dark spaces. When used in line and larger quantities they mark a walkway or indicate the direction one has to follow.

Directional wall luminaires

Directional wall luminaires can emphasize an area in a space. The up-light type can illuminate the ceiling to accentuate an intricate ceiling cornice or noticeable decoration.

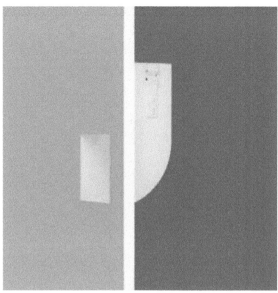

Figure 2.53 Recessed wall up-light. (Whitegoods)

Figure 2.52 Surface-mounted wall up-light. (Davide Groppi)

One can also shoot light in abundance against the ceiling, using it as a reflector to create a nice diffused light on the floor.

When directed downwards, wall luminaires act as floor-washers, highlighting the floor, guiding one along a corridor or lighting the steps on a staircase. Their unobtrusive and glare-free light makes them ideal for night-time guide lighting.

Another option for directional wall-mounted light sources are the lights on arms. Illuminating artwork, they are also fixed to desks or poke out of bed headrests, acting as reading lights. Luminaires on arms bring light where it needs to be with minimal glare and energy usage. They certainly form a niche in the vast array of luminaire products available. Most of them are decorative, while some blend better into the background.

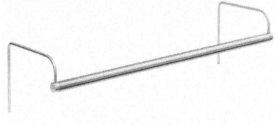

Figure 2.54 Wall-mounted directional picture light. (House of Troy, Slim-Line)

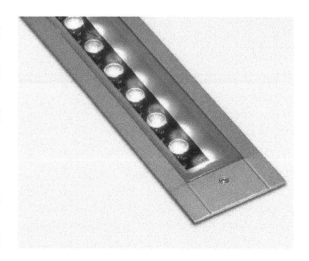

Figure 2.55 In-ground up-light with a deep-recessed light source. (Lightgraphix)

Figure 2.56 Linear LED in-ground wallwasher luminaire. (iGuzzini)

Floor-recessed luminaires

Floor luminaires often form the only element in an outdoor lighting scheme due to the lack of walls and ceiling. There are a range of surface-mounted luminaires, most of which are used in exterior lighting. Floor-recessed or in-ground luminaires, however, are also used inside. They are almost as versatile as ceiling-recessed luminaires. We have round or square point-sourced up-lights. They can wall wash, or accentuate a column with their narrow beam. We have the adjustable up-lights, allowing one to fine-tune and adapt the projection angle to changing circumstances. (It can, for example, follow a growing plant with its light, or simply indicate, as a set of marker lights, the way that has to be taken.) The in-ground linear range is almost as versatile as the point-sourced luminaire range. In-grounds used in interiors can add an additional layer and depth to a scheme. Their upwards shining light forms a nice contrast to light usually being projected downwards.

Unlike luminaires that are placed in the ceiling, floor-recessed luminaires are more likely to cause glare. As we walk, we humans tend to look more to the ground than towards the sky. When we pass by or walk over in-ground luminaires they can shine directly into our eyes. Glare protection like louvres

and deep-recessed light sources have to be considered when people are disturbed by the light source. Almost all in-ground luminaires are covered to protect the luminaire from dust and the user from the heat and electricity of the luminaire.

IP rating

Many floor-recessed luminaires are exposed to possible water and dust ingress. The lamp and particularly the electrical component have to be protected. The level by which a luminaire is protected from foreign bodies like water, dust or tools is called its ingress protection (or IP) rating. The rating consists of two-digit number. The higher the number, the higher the level of protection. The first number defines the level at which a luminaire is protected from solid objects while the second number describes its protection against water penetration. So IP00 offers no protection while IP68 offers the highest protection possible.

The position of the luminaire determines the level of protection needed. Luminaires positioned very high up require the protection because a sealed luminaire will inevitably work for longer and this positioning would make the need for regular maintenance undesirable. Luminaires in wet locations need the protection for the very same reason but

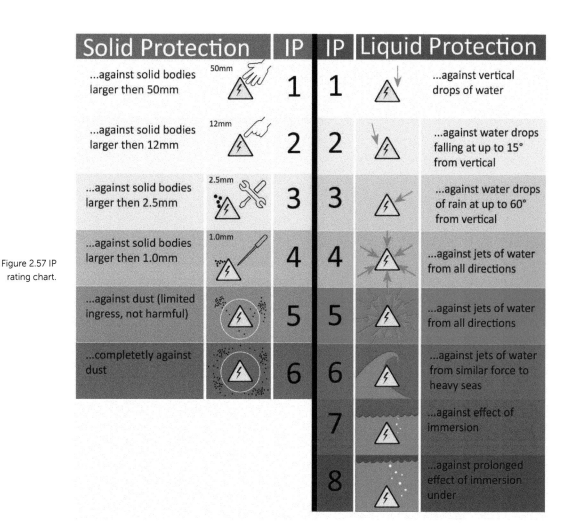

Solid Protection		IP	IP		Liquid Protection
...against solid bodies larger then 50mm	50mm	1	1		...against vertical drops of water
...against solid bodies larger then 12mm	12mm	2	2		...against water drops falling at up to 15° from vertical
...against solid bodies larger then 2.5mm	2.5mm	3	3		...against water drops of rain at up to 60° from vertical
...against solid bodies larger then 1.0mm	1.0mm	4	4		...against jets of water from all directions
...against dust (limited ingress, not harmful)		5	5		...against jets of water from all directions
...completetly against dust		6	6		...against jets of water from similar force to heavy seas
			7		...against effect of immersion
			8		...against prolonged effect of immersion under

Figure 2.57 IP rating chart.

more importantly because of the health and safety of the user. Luminaires inside a pool need therefore an IP rating of 68. Luminaires in an open garden or terrace should have an IP rating of 67. The IP rating in the bathroom depends on the position of the luminaire in comparison to the water. As this varies, so the IP rating is split into three zones. Zone 0 is the area inside the bathtub or shower tray and requires the highest protection. Luminaires in this zone should have an IP rating of at least 67 and have to be run at 12v. Luminaires within Zones 1 and 2 require an IP rating of at least 44. If water arrives at pressure, an IP rating of at least 65 is required. For luminaires positioned in Zone 3 there is no need for IP rating.

CONTROLLING LUMINAIRES

What is a lighting control system?

The conventional way of controlling light in a room is the standard light switch. Each light or light group is controlled by a single on/off switch or dimmer switch. The more light groups, or so-called lighting circuits in a room, the more switches are necessary. Imagine having five switches in a room – achieving the desired light effect would quickly become inconvenient, if not annoying.

Lighting control systems allow you to enter a space, turning all lights on, creating the desired lighting effect at the push of a button. A keypad/wall

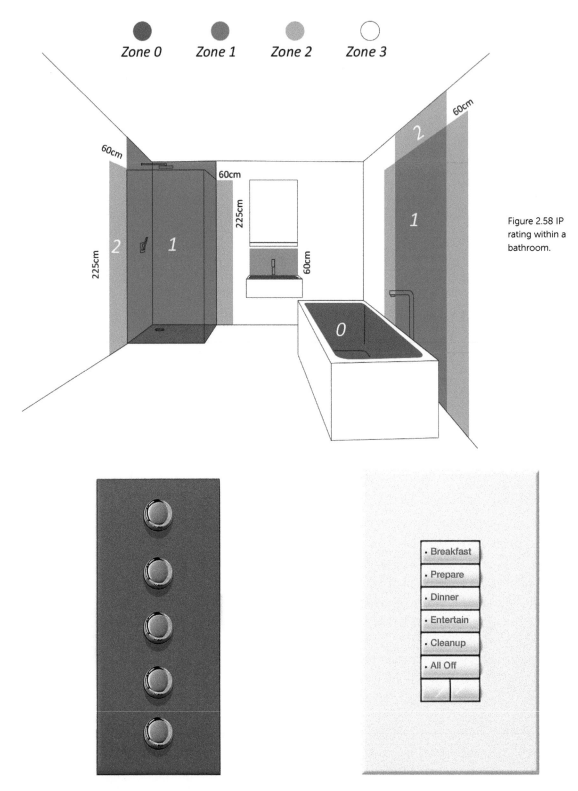

Zone 0　　Zone 1　　Zone 2　　Zone 3

60cm

60cm

60cm

225cm

225cm

60cm

2　1

2

1

0

Figure 2.58 IP rating within a bathroom.

Figure 2.59 Standard wall-mounted dimmer switch. Each light can be turned on and off separately.

Figure 2.60 Lutron keypad/wall station, which turns various lights on to a set setting or 'scene'.

• Breakfast

• Prepare

• Dinner

• Entertain

• Cleanup

• All Off

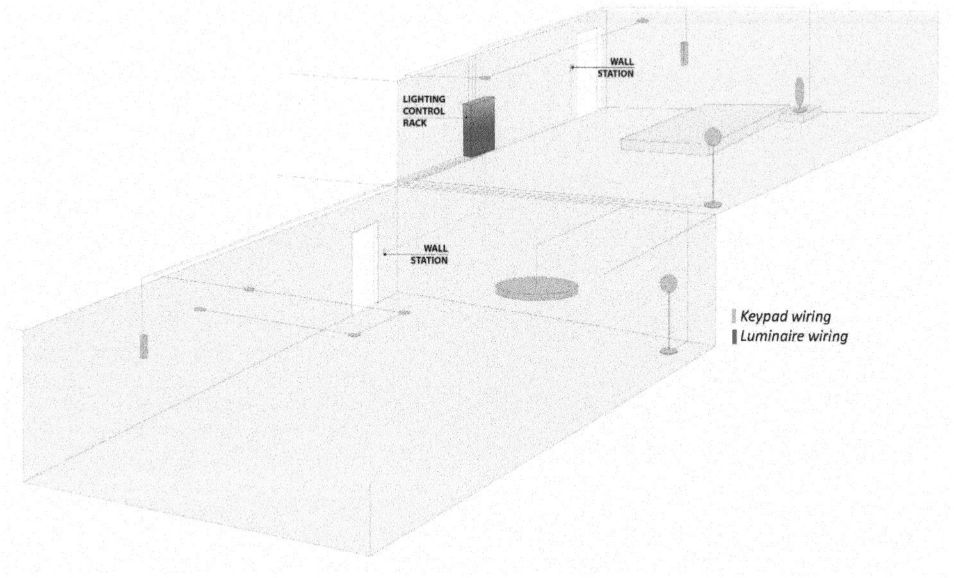

Figure 2.61
Schematic of a house with a central lighting control. Luminaires and keypads are wired separately and end in the lighting control rack.

LIGHTING CONTROL RACK

WALL STATION

WALL STATION

| Keypad wiring
| Luminaire wiring

station replaces the light switch and offers you various scenes. Each scene sets the various luminaires into a different setting thereby creating different moods.

This requires all lighting-related cabling of a space or a house to end in a single place. This can be a cavity in a wall or a small service room. This is where the lighting control rack sits. It sets the requested light levels of a scene when it receives a signal from either the wall-mounted keypad, a remote control or an iPad.

Do I need lighting control?

The short answer to this would be 'Yes!'. Lighting control is an essential part of every lighting scheme.

Figure 2.62 Three different lighting schemes. (Corpus Christi Church, Brixton, London)

■ *circuit 1* ■ *circuit 2* ■ *circuit 3* ■ *circuit 4*

Figure 2.63 Various control circuits in a restaurant – colour-coded.

What are control circuits?

The two main factors to be considered in a lighting control scheme are the amount of circuits and the control methods. Control circuits define all luminaires one would like to control at the same time. Say, for example, all down-lights in a space are grouped and react simultaneously to the control signal of the lighting control rack. The more circuits there are, the more control ports within the control rack are necessary. Each control circuit needs at least one port. There is a limit to how much wattage a circuit or a port can handle. If the wattage exceeds the allowed load the circuit has to be split and two ports are necessary.

What is a control method?

There are various ways a light source can be controlled. The control method depends on the lamp type and project type. Each control methods occupies one port within the lighting control rack. If one has three different control methods running on the same control circuit, three ports are required. The control system can treat them as one group despite them occupying various ports.

Control method: on/off

The easiest way to control a light is to simply switch it on and off. A relay within the lighting control rack turns the light on or off – dimming the luminaire is not required. Additional control cables are not necessary here.

Control method: mains dimming

Mains dimming is also known as trailing-edge and leading-edge dimming. In this chapter, we have learned the differences between these two dimming/control methods. To make sure the light source gets the right type of dimming one has to make sure the

It not only allows one to fine tune the light levels to achieve the desired lighting effect, but more importantly it can change the perception of a space dramatically. Controlling the light allows one to change the focus from one part of the space to another or limit the focus on a small area rather than the entire space.

Whether and to what extent lighting control is necessary not only depends on the budget and size of a project but also on the type of project. A decent residential project can require a complex control system as one has to allow scenes for each room in a house. The same size open-floor office or retail space, on the other hand, will require fewer scenes. They use fewer luminaire types and fewer circuits than residential projects. This makes the control easier and the square metre cost therefore more affordable when compared to residential projects. The number of different luminaire types in a residential house, each requiring a different control method, makes the control more challenging.

right method is stated in the Specification and Load and Control Schedule. The degree to which the lamp is dimmed is defined by the intensity of the alternating supply current. This means that here too there is no additional control cabling necessary. The two cables running from the control rack to the luminaire are sufficient to allow for dimming.

Control method: 1–10v dimming

1–10v dimming is an analogue dimming method. Unlike the previous control method, this method requires two additional low-voltage wires running from the control rack to the driver or ballast. These wires supply the driver with the DC control voltage.

The maximum control voltage of 10v applied makes sure that the light source runs at 100 per cent while 1 per cent dims it down to a minimum. The same applies to the 0–10v dimming with the difference that the 0v control current turns the light source off and no additional relay is necessary. Both 0–10v and 1–10v dimming are simple to install and run. They are an effective and safe way of dimming luminaires. The additional cabling has to be considered and does add cost. When it comes to huge and complex projects it gets replaced by the following control methods.

Control method: DSI then DALI

DSI stands for Digital Serial Interface and is a system introduced by the driver manufacturer Tridonic. A single manufacturer holding all licences means that one remains restricted when it comes to ballast and driver choices. Just as with 1–10v dimming, DSI requires two low-voltage DC control cables. There is no polarity for the control cable, which reduces installation errors. As it is a digital system, it allows a computer to address and control luminaires centrally. The fact that it is computer-controllable makes it attractive for bigger buildings. If one wishes to join various luminaires to a control group this must happen by hard wiring. DSI is often referred to as the basis for DALI system and has been replaced by its successor DALI.

DALI has been developed by several manufacturers. Their aim was to create a system that allows their lighting equipment to connect together. It is a very powerful data protocol as each luminaire can be controlled separately. One can group luminaires by programming rather than hard wiring. This makes this control method extremely flexible. Wiring is less complex compared to DSI and 1–10v, making it

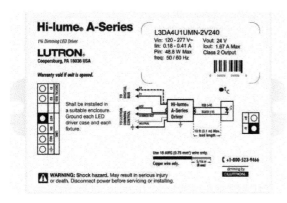

Figure 2.64 1–10v dimmer with two additional ports for the low-voltage control wires (Lutron).

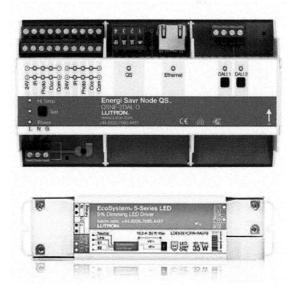

Figure 2.65 (Above) Dali driver. (Below) DALI controller for sixty-four drivers and ballasts.

more cost-effective in the installation phase. A single DALI controller can address up to sixty-four ballasts and drivers, which makes the actual control unit cost affordable. DALI requires pre-programming, and each driver receives an address number ranging from zero to sixty-three.

Drivers and ballasts can feed back if a light source is not working. This is the ideal system for big offices and commercial buildings. It is a system that is able to ease maintenance and lighting control in a building but also needs the knowledge of an expert when failures occur or re-programming is required. A failing driver, for example, needs to be located and given the same address number it had before.

Figure 2.67 DMX interface. (Lutron)

Control method: DMX

DMX512 is a digital communication standard that was used mainly in stage lighting. It quickly moved from the entertainment world into architectural lighting. DMX allows one to link lighting controllers to dimmers. The number 512 stands for 512 separate levels or channels. Each channel is dimmable in 256 steps. This fast control method is particularly suitable for controlling coloured light. Whether this is

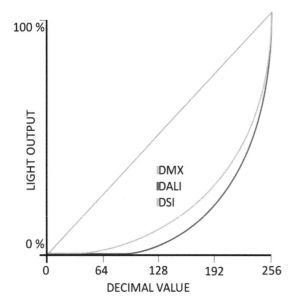

Figure 2.66 Dimming curve comparison.

RGB LEDS in giant media screens, tiny LED strips or dynamic white floodlights, DMX is *the* communication standard. RGB or dynamic white LED boards require more than one channel for control. The RGB LED needs three channels to control red, green and blue colours separately; the dynamic white LED uses cold white and warm white LEDS and requires therefore at least two channels for control. Unlike DALI, which has an exponential dimming curve, DMX dims all devices in a linear manner.

It is unusual to see a project where only one dimming method prevails. DMX is a control method that in architectural projects will work alongside a second control method. Whether this is DALI or 1–10v it complements a system when colour controlling is required. DMX converters or interfaces are therefore essential as they transform the DMX signal so it is understood by the lighting control system.

How to use these methods

The various control methods might at first sight appear confusing. How does all this fit together and what method should one choose? Obviously, the fewer control methods one chooses the better. The feedback option in a DALI system doesn't make it only interesting for huge office buildings and department stores. Small boutiques might want to go for a

DALI the system as it can be kept slim and inexpensive. It has to be programmed once, however, and if a change in the set-up is necessary, a specialist has to be consulted.

Many residential projects require various control methods and many circuits. Here mains dimming is often paired with 1–10v dimming as it is easier to maintain and re-program. If coloured lighting comes into play one has to allow for DMX interfaces. It is therefore not rare that a residential project requires a more complex control system than commercial buildings.

In all cases, space is required for a control panel that hosts all the control devices and splits the power into the various control circuits. A processor allows one to program and store the scenes for all the rooms and takes the orders of the various keypads in the house.

Keypads or iPads allow one to retrieve a scene independently from the location. A keypad is only signal-wired unlike a dimmer switch that is physically connected to the mains power and the luminaire. The keypad sends a signal to the power rack. The control panel switches and controls the luminaires in a room. This means that a keypad in the basement corridor can be programmed to control a light on the roof terrace if necessary. One can have light colours change automatically throughout the day, triggered by an integral astronomical clock. The combination of keypads, the internal processor and the astronomical clock of a lighting control system creates a powerful and extremely flexible tool to control light.

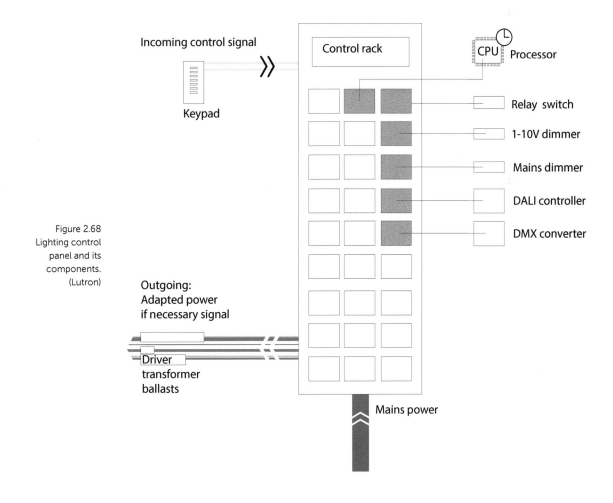

Figure 2.68
Lighting control
panel and its
components.
(Lutron)

Chapter 3

TREATMENTS AND TECHNIQUES

ONE CAN GET EASILY OVERWHELMED BY the many luminaire types and the endless possibilities they offer, so where does one start and what luminaires does one use?

The quickest way out of this dilemma is not to think about the luminaires but the effect that one wants to achieve. This chapter shows the basic lighting treatments and their effects. Going further, it shows the luminaires that are suitable for each treatment. Many lighting treatments or techniques depend heavily on the detail that the luminaire is placed into. The exact positioning and angle of the luminaire type will determine whether the envisaged treatment works well. The aim is to show the lighting treatment and its effect and purpose. If there are design details, they are shown in principle with a selection of luminaires for each treatment.

WALL TREATMENTS

Wall-washing

One distinguishes generally between two main wall treatments with light. One is wall-grazing and the other is wall-washing. The difference between these is often not fully understood. Wall-washing is when luminaires are positioned in such a way that their emitted light illuminates the wall evenly. The position and the angle of the luminaires don't create strong shadows. The aim of the light is to make the wall stand out. Often the walls contain artwork, corporate signage or other elements deserving to be highlighted. Light shining onto a wall that is painted in a

Figure 3.01 A smooth light effect created by a lighting technique.

particular light colour will bounce that colour onto the floor. If there is enough reflective light it can provide enough general light in a room to make additional lighting unnecessary.

A wall can be washed from the floor or more commonly from the ceiling. The light sources can be recessed or take the form of track-mounted spotlights.

One has to make sure that light reaches the very top of the wall and all the way down to the floor. To get a good and even wall wash it is crucial to maintain the right distance between each luminaire and from the luminaire to the wall. These parameters are different with each luminaire type and depend on the wall height. Shadows or scallops that occur when the distances are not right have to be avoided. The distance to the wall is also crucial when using linear recessed luminaires or luminaires hidden in a ceiling detail like a cove or slot.

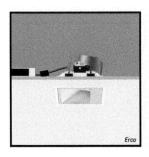

Figure 3.02 Typical point light source for wall-washing.

Figure 3.03 (Left) recessed linear luminaire. (Right) luminaire to go into a cove or slot. Asymmetric beam angle α is 30 degrees and β is 60 degrees for a linear wall-washing.

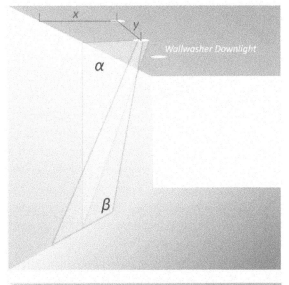
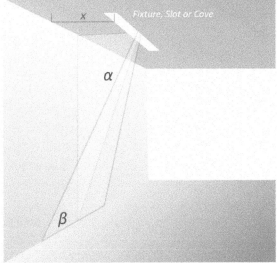

Figure 3.04 Wall-washing. The up/down throw angle α is different to the side throw angle β in an asymmetric beam angle. The distances x and y of the light source should take this into account.

The beam angle of the luminaire is asymmetric while the light sources or reflectors are angled towards the wall.

Wall-grazing

When grazing a wall with light, the luminaire is positioned close to the wall. The light shines towards the wall at a steep angle. This treatment creates stark shadows and is particularly suitable for accentuating textured façades, tiles or treated glass walls. Grazing a wall usually requires a recess detail that hides the luminaire. The recess can be positioned in the adjacent ceiling, wall or even floor. This type of treatment is not restricted to textured walls only. It can be applied to any surface that deserves to be highlighted. This can be an old stone wall, a wallpaper or photo wall. If a recess is not possible, surface-mounting the luminaire is an option. In this case, the light source should be hidden with a simple screen. This prevents one from seeing the luminaire and can avoid unwanted glare. Until recently, this effect would have been achieved by positioning many down-lights alongside a wall. This would have created a striking effect yet also produced many unnecessary scallops on the wall.

Today's lensed linear LED luminaires can create an even wall-grazing. The LEDs within the light fixture are positioned close to each other and point downwards. The asymmetric beam angle is designed

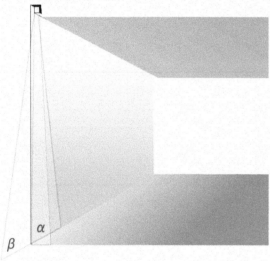

Figure 3.05 (Above) conventional wall-grazing with a row of down-lights creating unwanted scallops. (Below) modern asymmetric linear LED wall-grazing without scalloping.

to push as much light downwards as possible, while the numerous closely pitched LEDs help to avoid scallops.

Attention should be given, however, when grazing a wall, to where the finish is not perfect as any unevenness or flaws in the wall will be exposed and highlighted. This treatment is not suitable for illuminating paintings. The deep picture frames will cast shadow onto the artwork when lit from this steep angle.

Figure 3.06 Surface-mounted linear luminaires for a cove or slot. A typical asymmetric beam angle for a wall-grazer is α15 x β60 degrees.

Wall bleed

Unlike the two previous methods, the wall bleed is not used to treat the entire wall with light. The light usually bleeds out of a ceiling recess illuminating only the area close to the light. The low intensity of the light and the detail are key in creating this effect. This draws one's attention upwards rather than onto the wall. Accentuating only the perimeter of the wall makes one aware of the proportions of a space without treating the entire wall. Wall bleeds work well in combination with other lights as they leave space for additional lighting on the wall. For example, spotlights can be set in contrast, highlighting a picture on a wall. A decorative wall-mounted luminaire can fill a gap on the wall if necessary.

To get the effect right, the detail needs to be right. Whether shielded by a cove, recessed or screened, the beam angle of the luminaires is usually wide. A controlled forceful light is not necessary but instead a soft, wide and ideally diffused linear light source can be used. Luminaires should have at least a 120-degree beam angle – the wider and the more diffused the better. This allows for soft light bleeding out of the recess or cove.

LED strips are often used and glued into built-in details. Once glued in, their position cannot be changed if the light effect is not as desired. The cabling is challenging and they can peel off if the surface is not clean or dust-free. It is therefore helpful to use luminaires that are designed for this purpose. The

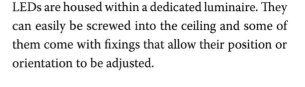

LEDs are housed within a dedicated luminaire. They can easily be screwed into the ceiling and some of them come with fixings that allow their position or orientation to be adjusted.

Edge lighting

Glass walls or partitions form a small yet important category within lighting treatments. It is worthless to illuminate glass unless it is treated. Light travels through clear glass without creating an effect as it doesn't have a surface to bounce off. To allow it to have an effect one needs to create a surface on which light can be refracted or reflected. Etched, fritted or printed glass gives light the needed surface.

The glass can be treated to create effects where the lighting effect is needed. If treated on the outside, the light source has to be outside. In this case, the only possibility to illuminate the glass is to graze it with light. If the surface treatment is laminated between two glass layers, edge lighting is in many cases the most effective and impressive way to illuminate the treated glass. It allows a lot of light within the glass to bounce off into the space. The glass appears to glow. The effect is heightened when the light source is hidden.

Wall-grazing fixtures with an asymmetric lens work well in edge lighting. They ensure that the effect is even and intense. In some cases where more punch is necessary, a symmetric, very narrow beam of light can be the right choice. It ensures that the light travels wider and shows more effect on the glass.

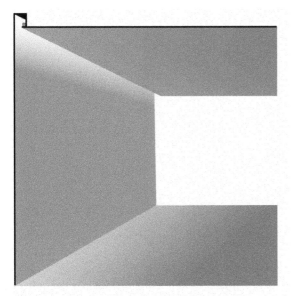

Figure 3.07 (Above) a subtle wall bleed only. (Below) a wall bleed with an additional luminaire on the wall.

KKDC

Vexica

EcoSense

EcoSense

Figure 3.08 Luminaires for cove lighting. When dimmed down, they create a soft wall bleed.

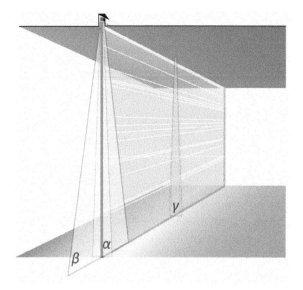

Figure 3.09 Edge-lit glass. Either to be lit with an asymmetric light beam α (narrow) and β (wide) or if the light needs to travel further down with an extra-narrow
(y = 10-degree) beam angle.

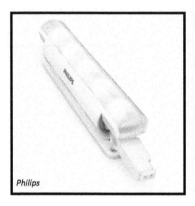

Philips

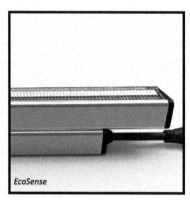

EcoSense

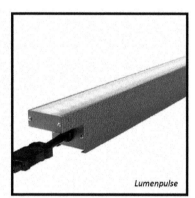

Lumenpulse

Figure 3.10 Linear LED luminaires with integral driver. The asymmetrical wall-wash lenses or very narrow beam optic make them suitable for edge lighting.

The fixtures should ideally be hidden which in many cases is a challenge. Often there is not enough space to recess them deep enough to avoid visibility. The use of louvres and grilles can help to disguise the luminaire from most viewing angles.

THE CEILING

Ceiling up-lighter

Providing a ceiling is interesting and free of any services, it can lend itself to being treated by up-lighting. The ceiling can be lit to highlight a defined area such as an entrance or act as a giant reflector, bouncing the light onto the floor and providing it with general light.

On both occasions, the ceiling is lit intensely. Depending on the ceiling height and ceiling colour, one will have to generate between ten and twenty times the light that later falls onto the floor and walls. It is not very economical to send light a longer way, bouncing off a ceiling to create general light in an area. The quality of that light differs from that of direct down-light. It includes the ceiling while delivering light on the floor. This is not always desired. Ceiling up-lighting is often just used to emphasize a beautiful ceiling or arches and is then combined with additional lighting that provides the appropriate light level on the floor.

Ceiling up-lighting can be found everywhere that the ceiling warrants treatment with light. Up-lighting makes one aware of the height of a space and impresses the viewer. It is therefore used in churches, airports and entrance lobbies but can also be found everywhere that the ceiling is out of reach. Low-ceiling rooms profit from this treatment as it visually lifts the space.

The typical light source is a wall-mounted up-lighter with a wide flood beam angle. Alternatively, cabinets or other architectural elements can be used to conceal up-lighting luminaires. The luminaires need to be placed safely and the light source should not be visible to the eye of the observer.

Down-light arrangement

Unfortunately, not all ceilings are interesting or clean. Ceilings are often cluttered with all types of necessary services. They hold cooling/heating, sprinklers, smoke detectors and emergency signage often combined with a grid of down-lights. When placed in the space without coordination the ceiling tends to look busy and unattractive.

Architects and clients are becoming more and more aware of this. They are paying more attention to it and are looking to visually calm ceilings. This needs to happen in coordination with the lighting.

Figure 3.11 Ceiling up-light with wall-mounted or surface-mounted luminaires.

  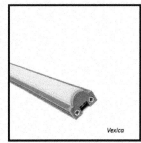 

Figure 3.12 When up-lighting, the fixtures need to be powerful and have a wide beam angle. Surface-mounted point sources are suitable as well as rows of linear LEDs with 120–290-degree light spread.

Figure 3.13 Undesirable cluttered ceiling.

Figure 3.14 Organized ceiling.

Does it really have to be all down-lights?

Today's lighting industry offers so many tools to treat a space with light. A combination of treatments is always the ideal solution as this allows us to tailor the lighting to the needs of the room. When done appropriately, the ceiling appears calm and all falls into place. If down-lights have to be used, apply the rule: 'less is more'. One should reduce the number of luminaires to the minimum possible by calculating how much light is actually required. Instead of twenty small down-lights, try to use eight more powerful luminaires. Down-lights can be arranged in arrays and grouped in lines or in a pattern. One should place down-lights only at locations where they are necessary rather than simply applying a grid. If possible, it helps to position the luminaires out of sight towards the perimeters of a space and group them.

Look at the entire space and try to establish relationships between luminaires' groups and architectural elements like columns, windows and partition walls. Arrange lights around these architectural elements and they suddenly become part of the space rather than an imposed template.

The choice of whether to use round or square

Figure 3.15 Round and square down-lights.

down-lights can be down to preference, but there are occasions when round down-lights are more suitable, for example, when they are arranged at an angle or when following curves. They are also more forgiving when placed in a grid. Square down-lights generally work better in right-angled rooms. They have the advantage of being perceived as a single fixture when aligned or arranged in groups.

Slots

Ceiling slots allow luminaires to be hidden and set out in groups at the same time. They offer the opportunity to combine lighting and other ceiling services like air-conditioning or sprinklers. This is an effective way to declutter the ceiling by creating more untouched ceiling space.

The fact that one is not able to see the light sources allows the use of more cost-effective fittings. When laying out the dimensions of a slot there is always an antagonism between recess depth and slot opening. A deeper slot hides the light source better. A wider slot allows the luminaire to tilt more and to cover a greater area.

The slot dimension and its final design depends on the available recess depth as it defines the choice of the luminaire. The position of the slot defines in what direction the luminaires are pointing. If the luminaires have to be able to point in all directions, one should use a standard slot.

The standard slot has enough space for a track-mounted spotlight. The track is positioned in the middle of the slot. The luminaire has to almost poke out of the slot. The track within the slot allows for maximal flexibility as luminaires can be added, exchanged and repositioned. The slot can be shallower if one requires the lights to be only adjustable and no other services are running in the slot. In this case, ceiling-recessed gimbals offer a good alternative to surface-mounted track spotlights.

Linear LED luminaires need smaller slots. They are often used around the periphery, treating walls. In all cases, the detailing and the positioning of the luminaire have to be approached carefully. The luminaire shouldn't spill light onto the slot when aiming at its target.

Beams, baffles and services

The rules in the previous pages apply for plain ceilings where the luminaires cannot be hidden.

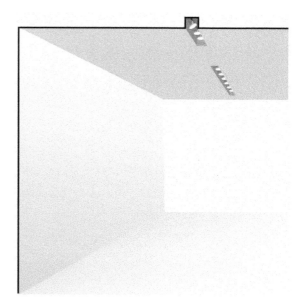

Figure 3.16 Adjustable track lights in a ceiling slot.

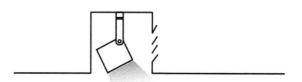

Figure 3.17 Deep slot with track light.

Figure 3.18 Shallow slot with recessed gimbals.

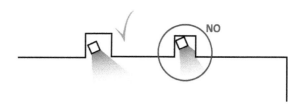

Figure 3.19 Smaller LED slot for linear LEDs. (Left) light exiting correctly and (right) light spilling onto the slot.

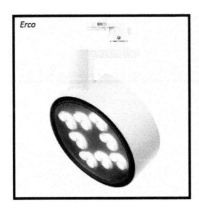 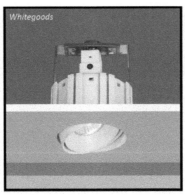 

Figure 3.20 Some examples of adjustable luminaires suitable for slots. A track light allowing for flexibility, a recessed gimbal guaranteeing a good finish and a linear LED for small slots.

Single-level ceilings are not always possible. For structural reasons, beams have to be introduced, and for acoustic reasons, baffles must be installed. To make maintenance easier, services are left exposed. Whether intended by the architects or not, obstacles allow lighting to be hidden.

The first impression of a space is the most important one. If beams, baffles and services are aligned at a perpendicular angle to the viewing point, they create the ideal opportunity to disguise luminaires. This can help to keep the ceiling visually calm. If luminaires are positioned properly, the fixtures shouldn't be visible but only the light they produce. The visibility of the fixture depends on where in a space one stands. The fixtures will be visible at one point so the selection of the luminaires is as important as when there aren't any structural beams.

What luminaire type to use depends on the finish and type of the space but also the position of the luminaire. A space with a high-end finish demands light fixtures with a nice finish. An industrial space with exposed services over various levels and a rough black paint finish is more forgiving. It allows us to hide fixtures more and copes better with more technical light fixtures as long as they come in the same colour as the ceiling.

Figure 3.21 Light hidden. (Above) a white finished ceiling with exposed beams. (Below) a busy ceiling with all services exposed painted in black.

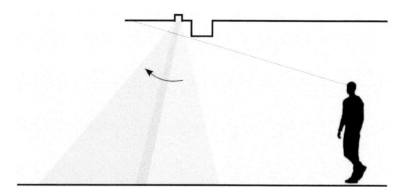

Figure 3.22 A beam disguising the luminaire. Adjustability limited to one direction to avoid light spill onto the beam.

Carefully select luminaires when locating them beside beams. The beam restricts the adjustability of the light to one direction only. One should make sure one can cover the desired area with light despite these restrictions. Light falling onto the beam when positioned too close to it or when aimed towards the beam should be avoided where possible.

THE WORLD OF COVES

A cove is defined in nature as a small sheltered bay. It protects a beach from the effects of strong waves and currents.

A lighting cove is effectively the same only that here the luminaire and its main accessories are shelters from visibility. The light that escapes through the

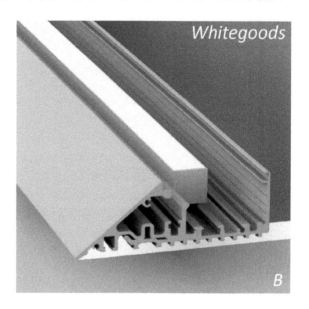

Figure 3.24 An extruded aluminium cove edge with a linear luminaire inlay.

Figure 3.23 A built cove with a linear luminaire inlay.

Figure 3.25 A curved extruded cove edge with an attached spotlight.

opening can be enjoyed without seeing the luminaire. Depending on where and how the cove is situated, it allows one to create very different effects, whether it is running vertically on the wall, creating a slot and allowing light to flow gently into the space or acting as a coffer flooding the room with light.

There are two types of cove: the standard cove with an upstand and the edge cove. When it comes to light performance there is no difference; however, they differ in appearance. In standard coves a vertical upstand guarantees that the light sources are not visible.

The edge cove prevents visibility through a sloped upstand. This creates a sharp and crisp finish and looks more contemporary. When positioned high up, the upstand is not visible and the cove ledge seems to have no edge.

Linear luminaires are positioned on the ledge. Their light bounces off the wall and ceiling into the space. All surfaces should be painted matte white. This will reflect more light into the space. If the illuminated interior is visible, the finish must be good.

Spotlights are attached to the cove profile or a track running inside the cove. They can be hidden entirely, allowing full flexibility paired with minimal

visibility. The cove should ideally be painted in matte black, the same colour as the spotlight.

Coves have traditionally been and are still mostly built by the contractor on site. There are, however, companies offering pre-manufactured cove extrusions for plastered ceilings. They can be ordered off the shelf and cut to measure. This is not only convenient and time-saving, it also guarantees good detail and the right light. A pre-manufactured cove product includes luminaires and ensures that the luminaires used are appropriate for the detail and can be positioned correctly.

The ceiling-to-wall cove

The ceiling cove when placed close against a wall provides good detail for a subtle wall bleed or a strong wall-grazing. This type of cove is more suitable when used with linear luminaires. The close offset to the wall hides the light source well. There is usually no need for an upstand, unless a reflecting wall makes it visible. This will affect the position and the type of the luminaires.

The same detail can create very different effects, depending on the type and position of the luminaire. A narrow-beam linear luminaire pointing downwards will graze the wall with light.

If one moves the cove far enough from the wall, one can wash a wall evenly with light.

A luminaire placed into the cove ledge pointing upwards will create a subtle light glow.

More indirect light can escape the cove when the inside of the cove is painted in matte white. The light of this up-lighting treatment with LEDs will need space to escape. Therefore, this type of treatment requires a minimum distance to the ceiling, depending on the luminaire type.

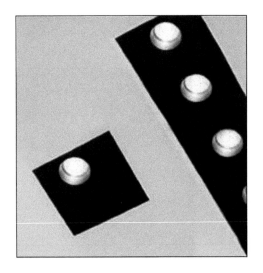

Figure 3.26 An adjustable spotlight in a recess created by coves. (Viabizzuno)

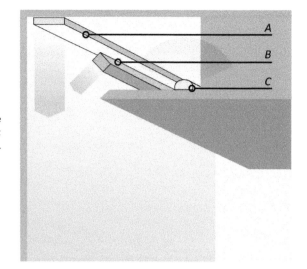

Figure 3.27 The light effect varies depending on where the luminaire sits and what luminaire is used. A = wall-graze; B = wall-wash; C = wall bleed.

Combinations and the 100mm rule

A ceiling-to-wall cove is only one of many possible positions for coves. They can be applied to all surfaces in a room – vertically in the middle of a wall or the corner of a room.

Light escaping from a gap in the wall feels more subtle and is more interesting than the light from a visible frosted plastic surface emitted by a linear recessed luminaire. It feels as if daylight enters the room through a gap.

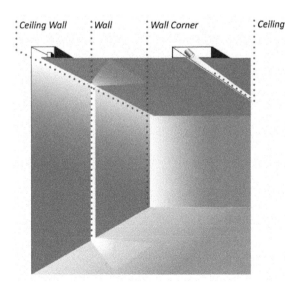

Figure 3.28 Positions of coves within a space.

When planning the detail, one should not only make sure that the light is not visible and the luminaires are rightly positioned but also that it is maintainable. The hand of the installer and person maintaining the luminaire needs to be able to enter the cove and exchange the luminaire elements. Off-the-shelf coves with clip-in luminaires can guarantee narrower gaps than conventional coves. A general rule of thumb is the 100mm builder's hand gap. This will allow enough light to flow out of the gap, hide the luminaire sufficiently and allow access if necessary.

Coffers

Ceiling coves positioned into a geometric form that up-light the recess they create are called coffers. They supply a room with plenty of indirect and diffused light using the ceiling as a giant reflector. The light they create is soft and uniform. The relative brightness of the ceiling is much higher than that of the floor. The brightly lit ceiling attracts a lot of attention and therefore demands a good finish.

Coffers can simply follow the geometry of a room, becoming a visually integral part of the space. But they can also define an area within a space. A round coffer in a rectangular space, for example, will stand

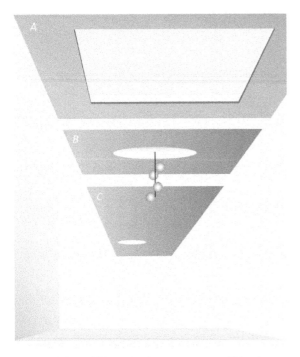

Figure 3.29 Coffer (a) following the room geometry (b) framing a chandelier or (c) marking an area.

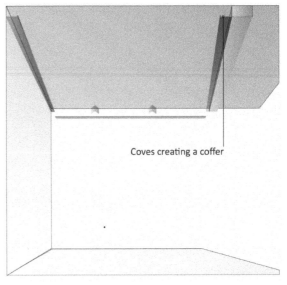

Coves creating a coffer

Figure 3.30 Coves can easily be attached to walls, ceilings and beams, creating a coffer.

out and can either mark out an area or indicate a change of direction. Coffers positioned around an object like a chandelier or a ceiling rose will frame and accentuate the objects they surround.

It is not uncommon that ceiling coffers are added to a space to highlight beautiful and intricate ceilings. They are easily attached to walls, ceilings or other architectural elements like beams.

Depending on the project type a coffer cove can be made of plain or decorative plaster cornice or a folded thin metal sheet. Depending on the light source, detail and effect wanted, each cove requires a different level of detailing. There are, however, four general rules that can be applied here.

1. The light source and ballasts/drivers/power supplies must be hidden. They are placed, therefore, behind the upstand of the cove ledge. This is essential because one can look into the coffer cove.
2. One should give the light the space that it needs to escape the cove. The further the light is from the ceiling the more light hits the ceiling directly. The effect on the ceiling is smoother and more light escapes. This is important if the cove is the main light source in a space.
3. Avoid showing a lamp image and get a continuous light flow. The right distance to the wall and ceiling are as important as the choice of light source. Test the chosen linear LED for the cove detail selected.
4. A white or light ceiling finish and rounded wall/ceiling edges help to push light into the space if necessary.

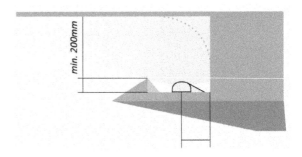

Figure 3.31 Typical detail for edgeless coffer and rafts.

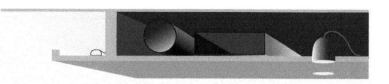

Figure 3.32 Rafts allow you to accommodate services.

Rafts

Rafts can be introduced to disguise other services like cooling, heating and acoustic absorbance. This is also a useful way to keep the other areas of a space clean and free of services, and to create higher spaces in other areas. The decision as to where the raft goes

Figure 3.33 Raft lowering the ceiling, separating it from the rest of the space.

has to be carefully considered and coordinated with all parties included in the project.

The raft can create a different atmosphere compared to other areas through colour, texture and, of course, lighting. Rafts can create a lowered, more intimate space. Just like coffers, ceiling rafts can accentuate an area, whether they are suspended over a bar or marking a product area within a shopping mall.

The coves in a raft are positioned to point outwards. The light shining outwards accentuates the boundaries of the space. The lowered ceiling creates recess space for additional lighting within the raft. One can look easily into the raft cove. The light sources within the cove have to be hidden well and the details carefully designed. As the area surrounding the raft is accentuated it should be kept free of ceiling services or other visual distractions. The lit ceiling finish has to be well executed. When detailing the raft, the same four rules apply that one has to consider when lighting coffers.

Some lights sources are better suited for use in coffers. Linear luminaires with a very wide beam angle, preferably emitting diffused light with a high light output, are ideal. They create a strong effect

Vexica

EcoSense

EcoSense

Figure 3.34 These luminaires are suitable for cove lighting. When dimmed down they create a soft wall bleed.

with a smooth light fade on the ceiling. Linear LED fixtures with a beam angle of 180° and wider tend to create a smoother light image on the ceiling

LIGHT PANELS

Light panels are an excellent way to elevate and enlarge a space. They produce a soft and diffused light, filling a space evenly with light. Whether placed on ceilings or walls, light panels can either dominate a space or, when architecturally imbedded, seamlessly integrate themselves into a space.

The 1968 movie *2001: A Space Odyssey* from Stanley Kubrick predicts a bright future, lit almost entirely with ceiling panels. It seems the movie prophecy was right here. Light panels are more popular than ever. Popular in galleries, generating an overcast daylight experience, they are moving into high-end shops and clubs. They have found their way even into our homes. Their diffused light creates a bright but soft light. This makes them ideal in work and play environments or in dressing rooms. Light panels have become one of the main features of our modern visual interior language. Together with the recessed linear luminaires and the cove they dominate today's minimal high-end living.

Standard light panels do need a lot of space. This is not feasible in an environment where ceiling depth is sparse. All services have to move around or behind a light panel. This requires planning and coordination of all parties involved. The light panel consists of a box and a diffuser material. The inner side of the box is painted matte white and holds the light sources and ballasts/drivers/power supplies. The distance between the light source and the diffuser panel has to be right to avoid a lamp image and to guarantee an evenly lit surface. The critical distance varies as it depends on the light sources and the diffusing material used; this will have to be tested in all cases.

The diffusing material ranges from etched glass and acrylic panels to stretched membranes. Which material is used depends the interior design, location, the size of the panel and the maintenance requirements. There are two types of light panel: the previously mentioned backlit panel where the light source is placed directly behind the diffusing panel and the side-lit panel.

Figure 3.35 Light panel finishing flush with the ceiling.

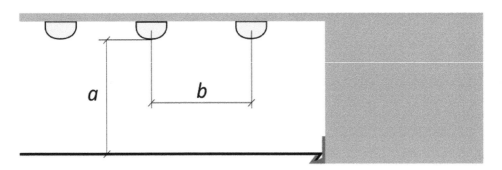

Figure 3.36 Standard light panel: stretched membrane in front of a light box. Luminaires are set at an ideal distance (a to b) to guarantee an evenly lit surface.

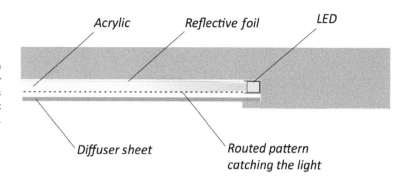

Acrylic   Reflective foil   LED

Figure 3.37 Side-lit light panel. The pattern on a side-lit acrylic panel will get evenly lit. The diffuser sheet or membrane sits in front of it and becomes an evenly lit surface.

Diffuser sheet

Routed pattern catching the light

Side-lit panels can be much thinner than backlit ones. They are restricted when it comes to surface size, light output and full integration of RGB and dynamic white.

This is because the light source is an LED strip placed around an acrylic sheet. The sheet is engraved in a pattern where light from the LED gets refracted. The engraved pattern is evenly lit. The lit pattern is then covered with the actual diffuser. Side-lit panels can be very thin and measure 30–50mm (1.2–2in) only. This is, compared to the 150–250mm (6–9.8in) of a backlit panel, a huge advantage.

LEDGE LIGHTING

Lighting from ledges is particularly common in refurbishment projects where the architects and interior designer reinstate an existing wall-cladding or add wall panels to the building fabric. In most of these cases, the ceiling can't be touched and it is worthwhile accentuating it with light. The ledge created by the wall panel is a good opportunity to hide luminaires, run cabling and host ballasts/drivers/power supplies.

The ledge size defines what treatment is possible. Linear up-lighters do not need a lot of space and are particularly suitable for narrow ledges. With the right luminaire and detail, the light illuminating the ceiling seems to come from nowhere. It is important to avoid creating hot spots of light on the wall and to create a natural light flow onto the wall and ceiling. The beam angle of the light and the way the

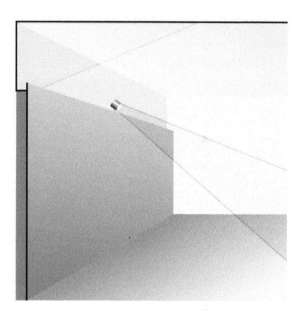

Figure 3.38 A ledge can be used to host up-lights or spotlights.

luminaire is positioned are crucial. Mock-ups are part of the process to guarantee that the lighting effect is as envisaged.

A ledge can hold adjustable spotlights, providing there is enough space. The spotlights allow one to accentuate elements within the room or to add more light onto the floor and tables if necessary.

The luminaires can be mounted onto tracks, mono points or simply be fixed with a bracket to the ledge. The size of the spotlight has to be coherent with the ledge size and the height. The higher up and the deeper the ledge, the bigger the spotlight can be. In some cases, it might be necessary to alter the ledge and add a small riser to disguise elements of a luminaire and its accessories.

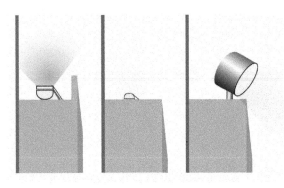

Figure 3.39 A. A powerful linear LED shooting light onto the wall and ceiling. B. A linear LED providing a subtle glow on the wall. C. A spotlight mounted to the ledge.

With a lower position, one has to be particularly careful when aiming the spotlights, considering the glare they might cause. Louvres, snoots and if possible a steep angle of the luminaires can help to minimize glare.

JOINERY LIGHTING

As the saying goes: 'The devil is in the detail.'

Joinery lighting is lighting integrated into furniture or other built-in elements in a space. The integration of light allows one to bring the light closer to the target. Literally all areas in a building where there is joinery and the possibility to supply power to it can be used to integrate lighting, providing there is sufficient space and, most importantly, the need for lighting in the area.

Joinery lighting is most commonly used in shelves where objects like books, art or products are illuminated.

Cabinets and room partitions in a space also allow one to integrate light. The joinery up-lighting of a wall partition sitting in the middle of a room

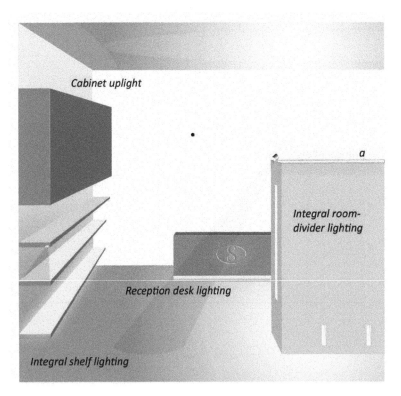

Cabinet uplight

Integral room-divider lighting

Reception desk lighting

Integral shelf lighting

Figure 3.40 The opportunities for joinery lighting are endless.

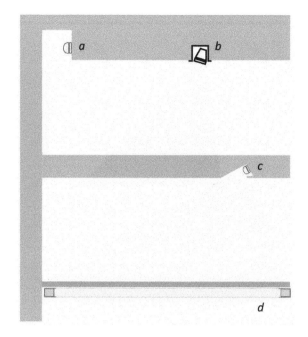

Figure 3.41 Just as in a normal space joinery lighting can host (a) Sots, (b) Downlights, (c) Coves and (d) Light panels.

creates a pool of light within the room, highlighting the area around it. The same partition can be used to integrate spotlights to accentuate elements in a space. Floor-washer or linear luminaires can be fitted into a cabinet. Joinery is the ideal light-distribution tool for certain areas in a space. Often the structure and surfaces of a building cannot be touched. In this case, joinery lighting becomes the only option to distribute light into the scheme. This makes this lighting method very popular in refurbishments projects. In most mid- and high-end shops, joinery shelf-lighting is a must as it highlights the products better than any other lighting. One can make sure that all products are lit equally and receive the accentuation desired. Shelves have, in effect, the same lighting treatment as spaces. One can introduce coves, slots, linears, light panels and spotlights. The same rules as for spaces apply here but in miniature.

Direct light sources should be hidden, glare avoided and the light level made accurate. In a residential project, joinery lighting can add new layers to the scheme, highlighting different levels and elements in a space. Whether integrated into the staircase, kitchen cabinet, reception desk or the window ledge – no other lighting method can add more sophistication to a lighting scheme than joinery lighting. There is nothing more intriguing than indirect light reflected off a material pouring into a space.

LOW-LEVEL LIGHTING

It is time to move from ceiling, wall and joinery lighting to floor or low-level lighting. Briefly mentioned already in Chapter 2, this treatment deserves more time and consideration.

We know from movies and theatre that lighting from below creates drama.

Lighting from a low level is, at the first sight, counter-intuitive. In nature, light shines either from above or the sides. Maybe because of that, low-level light draws attention when introduced into a space. It creates a very special atmosphere when used as

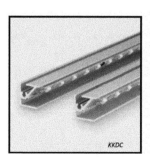
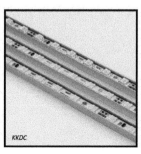

Figure 3.42 Some luminaires suitable for joinery lighting.

sole light source. There are two main methods in low-level lighting.

Up-lighting from the floor

Floor up-lighters are luminaires that are recessed or surface-mounted.

They illuminate either the walls or the ceiling of a space. Point-source up-lights are used to accentuate architectural element such as columns, window niches, etc. Up-lights create drama and draw attention where needed. They complement the lighting scheme by introducing luminaires at the opposite level.

In refurbishments, most ceilings are electrified already and covered with a plaster layer. This allows for easy manipulation and integration of luminaires.

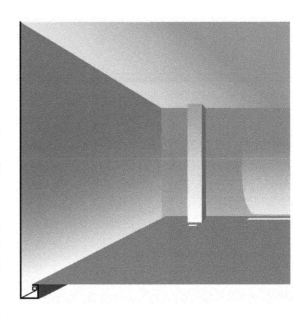

Figure 3.43 Opportunities for floor recessed uplighters. Laying into a slot or floor recessed.

Figure 3.44 Linear slot uplight and floor recessed uplighters, St Moritz Church. (Arch: John Pawson Architects; Lighting: Mindseye)

Luce&Light   *Lightgraphix*   *Lightgraphix*

Figure 3.45 Above examples for low level uplighting luminaries.

Many floors, however, are either wooden or tiled. Up-lights are, therefore, harder to implement. When installed, they face different challenges. They have to be able to resist water. Excess heat at the glass should be avoided to prevent one from getting burned when touching the luminaire. Depending on where floor-recessed up-lights are installed, the glass may need to be able to withstand weight pressure and be scratch-resilient. Glare is an issue with many up-lights, especially if they are placed where one can look directly at them. To avoid glare, one must use deep-recessed light sources and louvres.

Floor integral spot up-lights and linear up-lights are the usual way of distributing up-lighting. Due to their requirements, they often look very technical with a metal frame and exposed screws.

Some manufacturers have reacted to this tendency and designed nice-looking in-ground luminaires. Without the typical bezel these luminaires end flush with the floor, looking good even during the day when not in use.

Slots and coves don't rely on nice looking fixtures. Their look and performance depend on the designer's details, which allow one to disguise luminaires. One can create the same effects as with ceiling coves, from a strong grazing light to a subtle glow.

Figure 3.46 Indirect linear light bleeding out of a floor cove.

Floor-wash from the wall

Without doubt, floor-washers are not as dramatic as accent up-lights but they create a great mood light. While the up-lights draw your gaze upwards, accentuating the verticals and creating strong shadows, the floor-washers produce a more subtle and soft light on the floor.

Floor-washers rely on the absence of down-light or any other light that could lower their effect. One has to make sure the there is enough light/dark contrast to maximize the effect. Whether linear or point source they often indicate a path. Positioned in a corridor or on a path, they make sure the light level is sufficient for a safe passage. In a reception, they can mark an area around a reception desk. At home, they are the ideal night-light, giving you just enough light to guide you to the bathroom or welcome you when arriving

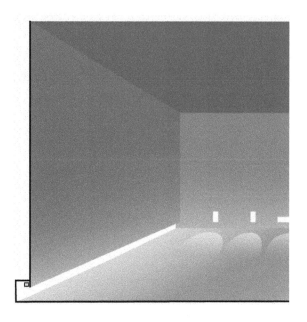

Figure 3.47 Linear wall cove or recessed treat the floor with discreet light.

Figure 3.48 Linear luminaires floor washing behind a skirting board, Eden Project Visitor Centre. (Arch: Grimshaw Architects; Lighting: Mindseye; Photo: Adam Parker)

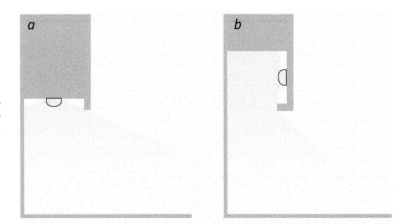

Figure 3.49 (a) Detail of matt and low reflective surfaces; (b) detail for a highly reflective floor surface.

home late at night. In clubs and spas, they create a pleasant low ambient light at the same time as making sure that movement through the space is safe.

Integrating floor-washers into walls is often challenging. It requires removing elements of the wall and supplying it with power before closing it again. It gets easier when luminaires can be recessed into cladding or a wall panel. Besides being able to use wall-washer luminaires for floor-washing, one can introduce a cove running alongside the floor. The detail looks similar to a standard cove. The lamps must be attached to prevent them from falling down but in effect all cove rules apply here. The spacing and positioning of the luminaire are similar to the standard cove.

The more space that is available, the more light that can escape. Matte white interior finishes to the cove allow more light to escape. One has to be mindful of the material used for the floor finish. Floors are unlike ceilings, and are often reflective due to the material used. Marble, tiles or polished stone, wood and concrete are shiny and can disclose the cove detail. Some glossy materials might be more forgiving than others and reflect less. Tests are inevitable if one wants to establish whether and to what extent the light source is visible. If the reflection is high then the light source will be fully visible. In this case, one has two options to avoid the visibility of the lamp image on the floor. Either one uses an opal diffuser on linear LED strips disguising their dots, or one hides the light source by creating an upstand similar to a coffer detail. This can affect the light output and must be considered especially in cases where the floor-washer is the sole light source.

Chapter 4

UNDERSTANDING THE PROJECT – WHAT QUESTIONS TO ASK

WHILST THE PREVIOUS CHAPTERS provide the basic technical knowledge of light, lamps and luminaires, this chapter deals with the effect that light has on a space, and the first questions one typically has when beginning a project.

Each of the main questions forms a sub-chapter and will be explained in further detail. All questions considered and answered should give us a good understanding of the essential light effects. Introducing the right questions usually eases the approach to more complex projects...

UNDERSTAND THE PROJECT

An important first phase within a project is to familiarize oneself with it. A project usually starts with a

Figure 4.01 How to design a gallery space that is interesting when not in use. EnBW Showroom, Berlin.

Figure 4.02 It is crucial to understand the cavities and gaps of a building. It allows us to determine where fixtures, cabling and transformers can be placed.

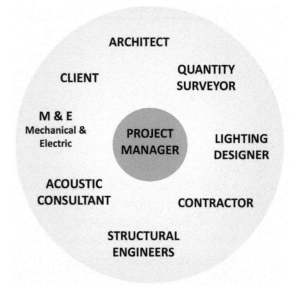

Figure 4.03 This diagram shows parties involved in a medium/large scale project. A lighting designer's closest relationship is typically with the architects and the M&E.

kick-off meeting where the client and architect share the plans, sketches, renderings or 3D files showing their design intent. If possible, one should visit the site to gain an understanding of scale and the characteristics of the building shell. A lighting designer will start to interrogate the fabric of the building, trying not only to understand the space but also what is beneath and above it. It is essential for our design to understand whether there is a false ceiling or if the walls and floors are solid or hollow. Knowing the recess depth of the surface and furnishings allows us to establish whether one can run cables to the various surfaces and whether the integration of recessed luminaires is possible.

A good meeting should make all the information available, but it is even better if this information can be supplied beforehand so the designer may familiarize herself or himself with it. Then the right questions can be asked, leading already to a first idea exchange and conceptual direction.

It would be great if one could walk off now and start designing, but first there are some essential points to consider.

Initial designs and rendering can be bold and pleasing to the eye but one starts to realize too often too late that not only the budget but also the timing on projects is limited. Sometimes guidelines are stringent and the allowed electrical load is challenging. In every case, working in a good team will lead to the best results. When all parties act in concert, problems are solved and a project profits on all levels from it, especially as we often share the space in the cavities of a building. Knowing the people involved and their position in the project is essential.

Of particular importance are the mechanical and electric engineers' (M&Es) heating and ventilation suggestions. They need to make sure that the heat the luminaires produce is cooled and will often need most of the hollow space made available by the architect. Therefore, good and open communications is of essence and is in many cases nurtured by a project manager. However, one should not wait until information falls into ones lap. It is essential to establish a good flow of communication by being proactive and understanding when and how to use the various communication tools like email, Skype or ones phone.

HIERARCHY: WHAT IS IMPORTANT?

One has to distinguish here between the project hierarchy and the aesthetic hierarchy. Each element within a building, whether it is of a decorative or functional nature, deserves attention and has its place, though some building elements have been given higher priority than others. Lighting is only one part of the various building elements and has to compete for a budget with others. When lighting is perceived as a technical rather than aesthetic element, it often doesn't get the attention needed.

During the architect's first presentation of the space, the design intent emerges. It soon becomes clear whether the designer/architect wants the space to look spectacular and extravagant or minimal and spartan, and what role the lighting has to play within this. It is easy for an experienced lighting designer to interpret the design and understand the visual hierarchies within the space, especially when accompanied by good plans, renderings and visuals. It is, however, not always clear what hierarchy the lighting has within the project.

It is therefore important to understand whether a project is driven by a small budget as this will put pressure on all aspects of the project, including the lighting. The same applies to energy requirements, which vary for each building type and zone – not to mention the various country or state regulations.

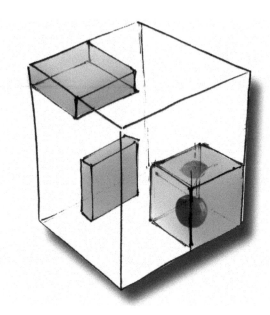

Figure 4.05 Cherry pick the areas. Prioritize to control budget.

To give an example: The interior redesign of a church where the overall budget of the lighting is 15 per cent of the entire project sets lighting in a different position than in a public building where lighting is allocated 0.4 per cent of the overall budget. In both cases, the energy requirement varies dramatically, allowing for more W/m^2 (watts per metre square) in the church than in a school or office building. Once one has understood these parameters, one can go ahead and start to prioritize areas in a building.

At this stage, the building can be split into treatment zones. The separation or zoning of the areas not only allows one to distribute budget but also to determine various treatments. It further allows one to address the desired lux levels and to consider the W/m^2 allowance.

As well as the aforementioned points, there are the aesthetic hierarchies of the building that should be considered as well, which at times conflict with the project hierarchies. If that is the case, it is important to be honest with the architect and client and raise the conflicts upfront to manage expectations and to establish a joint way forward. This allows us to

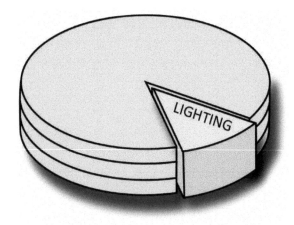

Figure 4.04 What is your part of the cake – cream or crumbs?

Analysis:
Zoning

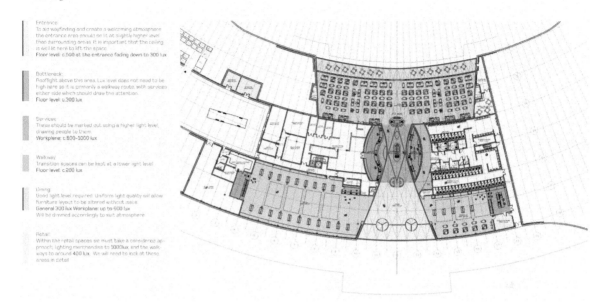

Entrance:
To aid wayfinding and create a welcoming atmosphere the entrance area should be lit at slightly higher level than surrounding areas it is important that the ceiling is well lit here to lift the space.
Floor level: c.500 at the entrance fading down to 300 lux

Bottleneck:
Rooflight above this area. Lux level does not need to be high here as it is primarily a walkway route, with services either side which should draw the attention.
Floor level: c.300 lux

Services:
These should be marked out using a higher light level, drawing people to them.
Workplane: c.500-1000 lux

Walkway:
Transition spaces can be kept at a lower light level.
Floor level: c.200 lux

Dining:
Good light level required. Uniform light quality will allow furniture layout to be altered without issue.
General 300 lux Workplane: up to 600 lux
Will be dimmed accordingly to suit atmosphere

Retail:
Within the retail spaces we must take a considered approach; lighting merchandise to 1000lux, and the walkways to around 400 lux. We will need to look at these areas in detail.

Figure 4.06 A zoning diagram example separating areas of a service station by treatment and light level requirements. (Glenn Howells Architects)

look at the aesthetic hierarchy, filtered through the project hierarchy.

One can now start to differentiate between the elements within a building/space that need to be fully highlighted, elements that can be highlighted and elements that must receive some form of light to comply with the lighting regulations.

A good example might be a representative reception linked by a glass façade and a glass door to the exterior.

A person wanting to enter the space will first try to establish whether it is open, then where the entrance is. Once one has entered, the eye wants to be drawn to the reception desk first. This establishes the first element of hierarchy within the reception – the reception desk. There are various ways to highlight

Figure 4.07 Corporate reception.

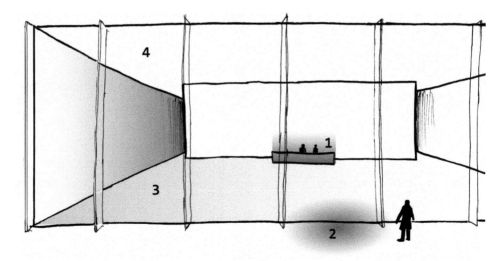

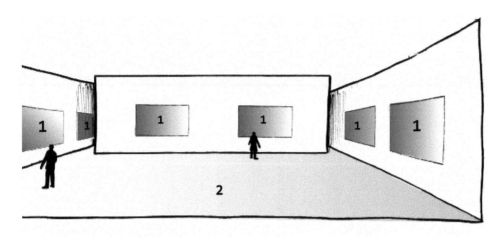

Figure 4.08 Low hierarchy – a gallery space inviting the viewer to wander around.

this and it doesn't need to happen with a lot of light. A visitor wants to see a person behind the reception desk. Now the visitor wants to see where to enter the space. If the architecture provides that information, the lighting can act as a supporting element; if not, light provides the most important information on where the entrance is located. Our entrance is therefore our second element within the hierarchy. We now have a very dark room with an accentuated reception desk and an illuminated entrance. One is not aware of the dimensions of the space nor of various elements and materials within the space. We have the core information but don't know how to get to the reception. We need a third hierarchy – the ambient light illuminating the floor and allowing us to move through the space in order to get to the reception desk. These three elements are the 'must' in our example; other elements are used to enhance the perception of the space. Often the fourth hierarchical element is the walls within the reception. A lit wall makes one aware of the scale of the space. Walls in receptions often become feature elements if texture, colour, the company logo or artwork is added.

While the artwork in a reception might end up last within the hierarchy, the artwork in a museum takes the prime role, followed by the secondary ambient light providing a safe light level by which one can navigate through the museum.

Often, light bouncing off the artwork and walls provides enough light by which to navigate and no additional light sources are needed. The main aim in a museum is to encourage one to stroll through it by creating a flat hierarchy. This has led to a movement in museum lighting where hierarchy in lighting is removed completely. Illumination is provided by a flat diffused lit ceiling, offering a uniform light simulating an overcast daylight that treats all surfaces equally.

Whether the hierarchy is flat, simple or complex, it is down to the lighting designer to determine how vertical and horizontal surfaces and objects will eventually interact in the space when exposed to artificial light. To guarantee a good lighting scheme, one will often have to add a layer to the necessary functional hierarchy elements to allow a balanced composition.

Part of that composition and a sure way of making a great difference is the way surfaces are treated in order to make them interact harmoniously. The decision as to whether to illuminate an entire wall or just the artwork can make a vast difference and has to be considered carefully.

WHAT PERCEPTION OF DEPTH DO I WANT?

Once the hierarchy within a space has become clear, one is inevitably faced with the question of the perception of depth. How do I want the place to feel? Do I want the space to appear high, wide, deep or shallow?

The human field of vision is designed to perceive vertical surfaces like walls or a room divider more strongly than horizontal surfaces like floors and

Figure 4.09 Front figure illuminated.

Figure 4.10 Back wall and left-hand figure illuminated.

ceilings. Vertical illuminance helps to define a space, as one can use that preference to manipulate the perception of depth when selectively treating surfaces with light. By doing so, one draws the attention of the eye onto a lit surface that becomes our point of reference. An object treated with light near to us, keeping the surrounding areas in relative darkness, will therefore make the space appear smaller as it limits the realm of visibility.

In contrast, a surface or object treated with light at the end of a room will draw our eye towards it, increasing our perception of depth. Any lit object there will appear bigger than an unlit object placed beside it.

The same applies to the remaining surfaces. An unlit low ceiling will appear oppressive. If this is not the intention, up-lighting can visually raise the ceiling, making it appear higher than it is.

In this case, the walls will need be lit less intensely to draw attention toward the upper area of our field of vision. In this way, treating the various layers that are available enables one to manipulate where

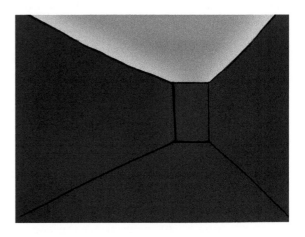

Figure 4.11 Lighting the ceiling lifts the space visually.

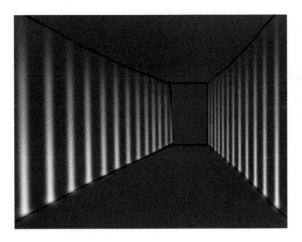

Figure 4.12 Rhythm created by uplight grazing the wall emphasizes depth.

Figure 4.13 Depth emphasized by linear luminaire composition.

attention is drawn to, thus creating depth, height or width.

Depending on the space, treating entire surfaces might not always be possible but the positioning of luminaires in a repetitive manner can have a similar effect or support the aforementioned effects. Luminaires positioned alongside a wall create a rhythm, dividing the wall into many entities. This magnifies the effect of depth as it adds a sense of relation. One can amplify the effect by knowing the laws of perspective whereby objects in a line leading away appear smaller and closer to each other the further away they are. The perceived intensity of the light decreases as well the further away a light source is, meaning that if one alters the rhythm, intensity and size of the light the perception of depth can either increase or decrease.

The aforementioned treatments are mainly the result of light reflecting off surfaces. On the other hand, the light source itself can achieve a similar effect. For example, the alignment, position, composition or shape of light sources within a space can support and accentuate the perception of depth or height.

Light fittings not only emit light into their surroundings, if they are visible they create a strongly noticeable pattern that can influence the way we experience a space. Therefore, one must be aware of the strong impact that visible light sources have in how we perceive a space. Their position, shape and pattern has to be chosen sensibly.

As with everything, there is a limit to what is achievable. At the end, the choice one takes has to relate to the architecture and the design intent and not attempt to work against it. A long corridor, for example, will remain a long corridor. The choices we make in what surface and area to treat will have to depend on their function. The hierarchy will determine the selection of our treatment. If the corridor leads to many hotel rooms, the entrances and the lift will automatically be very high in our hierarchy. If that treatment creates a depth already and we want to emphasize it, the aforementioned treatments can help.

WHAT CONTRAST RATIO DO I WANT?

Both hierarchy and depth perception depend on contrast of darkness and light. Objects and surfaces do stand out if the adjacent surface or area appears darker. Light contrast is created by light falling on surfaces, objects and areas, creating a noticeable difference in brightness. The word noticeable might be subjective but varies between us only marginally. A

Perceived distance	Illuminance Ratio
Noticeable	1.5 : 1
Distinct	3 : 1
Strong	10 : 1
Emphatic	40 : 1

Figure 4.14 J.A. Lynes' Perceived Contrast Ratio.

luminance ratio of 1.5:1 is perceived as noticeable (J.A. Lynes, 1987), while a ratio of 10:1 is perceived as strong.

The stronger a contrast ratio the more dramatic a scene will appear. In lighting, high contrast is mainly used in theatres and shop windows but also in museums and projects where ones view needs to be orchestrated to attract attention towards an area but also to disguise other areas.

Light contrast can be influenced by colour. Imagine a small room painted in matte white and illuminated by a single spotlight. The light will bounce off the walls, adding light to the surfaces, decreasing the light contrast.

An object illuminated within a black matte room by a single spotlight will stay in a starker contrast to a white surrounding. Black surfaces do not allow light to reflect and create spill light that can soften the contrast – it keeps the light effect where it happens.

The same applies to a large or open space where a single spotlight hits an object – the reflected light will lose its intensity when it hits the faraway wall; it will not add much light to other areas, thus not softening the contrast.

The perfect example of the aforementioned situation is the illumination of the £50 million diamond skull of Damien Hirst in the White Cube Gallery, in Mason's Yard, London. The small exhibition space, including the corridor, has been covered in black

Figure 4.15 Light-coloured environment allow for less contrast.

Figure 4.16 Dark-coloured environment help to create contrast.

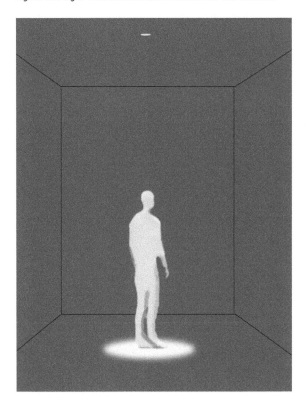

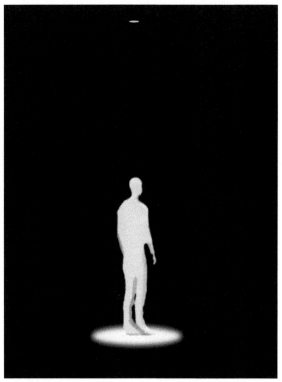

Figure 4.17 A huge light-coloured room has a similar contrast intensifying effect as a dark coloured room.

velvet to allow the eye to adjust to the darkness. Narrow-beam light sources pointing towards to the diamond scull result in an emphatic contrast of over 500:1. A person entering the space will perceive only the diamond skull as the main point of interest while the close-by walls disappear visually. The two security staff in their dark uniforms standing in the corner are not visible.

These extreme light conditions can be tiring to the eyes. Working in a high-contrast environment forces the eye to constantly adjust to the various light levels by dilating and contracting the pupil, soon leading to eyestrain. Therefore, the light in an office environment dictates a low-light contrast to ensure a long concentration period. It is recommended that a working surface illumination ratio with the nearby walls and ceilings is below 7:10 or >0.7. If these guidelines are applied slavishly throughout a space it will not only lead to a bland lighting scheme but also increase the overall energy consumption. Open office areas often include pantries, breakout areas, storage and waiting lounges, which allows one to zone the space to introduce various light and uniformity levels.

The two examples on contrast, mentioned previously, might be common but both are extremes. A well-balanced interior lighting scheme where hierarchies are desirable will have to be designed to a 1:3 ratio minimum and not exceed a 1:20 ratio.

WHAT LIGHT LEVEL DO I WANT?

Knowing what contrast one wants to achieve leads inevitably to the question of what light level or illuminance is required/desired and in some cases whether the light levels conform to the local guidelines. The local guidelines in Britain (CIBSE) set required light levels and permitted energy consumption per square metre that can vary radically depending on the space to be illuminated, allowing us in some cases more freedom in design than in other cases. We explain at the end of this chapter what lux levels are and what values are recommended in particular areas. The light levels mentioned in the guidelines apply mostly to horizontal surfaces and often exclude the vertical surfaces. Soulless lighting schemes will seek to fulfil the level requested by clattering the ceiling with a grid of down-lights. They will project most of their light onto the floor, guaranteeing an energy-efficient and uniform lighting scheme. This leads to lack of hierarchy, contrast and illuminated vertical surfaces within a space. So, starting with the light levels is lighting design the wrong way around.

Figure 4.18 Spill light of the illuminated artwork supplies enough light for circulation, Annie Leibovitz Exhibition. (Arch: Theis and Khan; Lighting: Mindseye)

The light level can fall into place effortlessly once we have established our hierarchy and we know what contrast we want to achieve. The treatment of the different surfaces will have the side effect of reflecting light onto the floor. In many cases, the light bouncing off the walls will throw a decent amount of light onto the floor, helping us to achieve the necessary light levels.

Sometimes this approach requires very rough lighting calculations at an early concept phase, but they are necessary if one wants to understand where and how much light needs to be supplemented. Adding light only where it is missing reduces the overall number of fixtures in the ceiling, leading to fewer visible light sources while leaving more ceiling untouched.

Hierarchy can often define light levels that are higher than the guidelines suggest, spilling additional light into other areas of the room. It is common that by treating the areas defined in the hierarchy one creates enough light-spill to fulfil the lighting-level requirements for the entire space. If the design intent is to create a higher light level one can now add light targeted at increasing the illuminance purposefully.

Light levels are a powerful tool in defining where and how long people choose to remain in a space. Ever wondered why fast-food chains choose a brightly lit space while other restaurants do not? Why some businesses use harsh direct light while others use soft indirect light? Direct light and high light levels in restaurants will expose us and put us into the spotlight – during a moment like eating or drinking that many

Figure 4.19 High uniform light level ensures a short stay.

of us choose to do privately. Therefore, providing high light levels over seating areas placed in front of a big window will guarantee that people move on quickly.

On the other hand, the same light in another environment, like a supermarket, has a different effect. Here, the supermarket profits from high, direct and uniform light levels. It makes sure that all products are presented equally and non-exclusively – helping us to 'hunt' more efficiently. Even the narrowest aisle is lit more than sufficiently, enabling us to read the small print on the cans. The bright light levels wake us up and make us aware of all the offers at the same time. The amount of information we are exposed to is not filtered by light, thus hindering quick choices and causing us to stay longer and consume more.

Figure 4.20 Typical bright uniform store illumination.

Selection and hierarchy are not created by deliberate variations in light levels but by product positioning. The more profitable products are usually positioned better, often at eye level where they are easier to spot and receive more light than the products on the bottom of the shelf.

DO I NEED AN ADAPTATION OR VISUAL BARRIER?

Have you ever turned on the bathroom light in the middle of the night? The sudden light-level change makes one close ones eyes almost automatically until one gets used to the light. When the light is turned off again everything plunges into darkness and seems darker than before.

This is because it takes the human eye up to half an hour to adapt from sunlight to complete darkness. The adaptation of the eye back to sunlight, on the other hand, takes only five minutes. Surely this has to be considered when designing with light? It is therefore common practice to allow for a gradual light change in larger buildings. In bright daylight, the reception of a museum or theatre might have the highest light level. Levels can then be lowered gradually from room to room, allowing the eye to adapt to darker conditions if needed.

Good architects, designers and curators know how to stage their spaces and exhibitions by introducing several rooms or partitions, allowing a gradual adaptation of light if needed. Lighting designers can then set the light level needed.

Beside the gradual adaptation, there is the 'comparative adaptation'. This is where a space has to compete with exterior brightness and therefore adapt to it. Shops will paradoxically have to raise their light levels during the daylight, so they do not appear too dark when compared to a bright sunlit street. This applies to all spaces where the external view and perception is of importance.

Short road tunnels, for example, are illuminated brighter during the day than in the night. The aim is to lower the light contrast between outside and inside, and to soften the transition for the eye.

On the other hand, a long tunnel in complete darkness without a visible exit would most certainly be perceived as an unknown and an obstacle. A person

Figure 4.21
London's Barbican
Art Centre entry is
illuminated brightly
by a large light
installation easing
the transition
from bright
environment.
(Arch: AHMM;
Lighting: Mindseye;
Photo: Andy Spain)

Figure 4.22 BMW Showroom, London designed to adapt its light level to the daylight. During the day high general light level, in the evening the light level is set lower. (Arch: Carbondale; Lighting: Mindseye)

approaching the complete darkness would most certainly hesitate to drive into it at 100kph (60mph). The unlit tunnel would be perceived as a black wall. A contrast of 10,000 lux to almost zero lux is an extreme example, where absence of light and contrast create uncertainly and a visual barrier. Most people tend to avoid darker areas when they can stand in a pleasantly lit space. Knowing the effect this has gives one a powerful tool in directing people, and creating zones of stay and unease.

DO I NEED WAYFINDING?

We all know that a sophisticated wayfinding system within a building helps to navigate. Most modern airports and metro systems use actively or passively lit signs to direct people. The right position, size, font and colour of signs helps to do this more efficiently. The light in these environments plays a supporting role. One has to make sure that the surface of an actively lit sign is lit evenly from within. All passive signs will need to be illuminated sufficiently to ensure a good visibility.

In a building where one wants to reduce signage to a minimum, lighting plays a key role in guiding people. Feature lights, for example, are placed to lead you in and to make you stop. They typically break the rhythm of a ceiling, subconsciously suggesting a change in direction.

The contrast of relative dark zones and lit surfaces and the transition between them can now help to direct ones vision and ease wayfinding within a building. We have previously explored the use of hierarchy to determine position of light. In most cases the right application of this method will lead

Figure 4.23 London's Barbican Art Centre. Circular coves indicate change of direction/decision point.

to a lighting arrangement that directs people and helps in wayfinding. Lit surfaces are a prime medium for directing people's vision and influencing their movement. Illuminating material, and the texture and colour of surfaces will visually stimulate some areas while others are deliberately neglected. A person standing in front of two corridors, of which one is lit while the other isn't, will prefer the lit corridor. Lighting invites people to enter a new space or puts people off. Not just any lighting within a corridor will work. The law of inertia says that a body in motion wants to remain in its current state. The same is true of a human moving through a space with regards to light. We tend to want to remain in the same lit environment. A sudden drop or increase in light is perceived as undesirable. A gradual light change is what we prefer.

On many occasions, wayfinding based on varying surface Illuminance is not possible. A more graphical approach like a continuous line of light will achieve a similar if not better effect. The light is almost perceived as an arrow line to be followed.

If one were to compare approaches in directing vision, none of those mentioned so far would stand a chance against curiosity. Interesting and stimulating effects addressing our sense of beauty or curiosity draws people more than any other form of lighting. Colourful light is perceived by many as the strongest attraction.

Figure 4.24 Showing how light guides and how darkness pushes off. A. Attracted by light. The desire to move towards the lit space. B. Pushed off by the darkness. C. Light intermediates between the lit and the dark spaces at the end of the corridor.

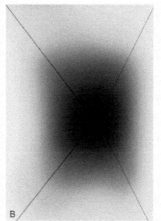

Figure 4.25 A light in the corridor invites the visitor to enter and proceed, Eden Project, Visitor Centre.

DO I NEED COLOURED LIGHT AND SUPERSATURATION?

Coloured light has certainly enjoyed a moment in the sun in recent times with the latest development in LED lighting. Never were coloured LED lights so cheap yet easy to control. Unfortunately, in too many instances coloured LEDs are used thoughtlessly. Too often, they are used on old buildings and structures without considering the natural attributes of the building. One sees on numerous occasions historic buildings deformed by bilious coloured light. There is no intention of accentuating the natural and original beauty of old weathered material. Colour is merely chosen to make the building stand out.

Coloured light is an extremely powerful tool and deserves sensible handling. A good example of the power of coloured light is the work of James Turrell. His installations dye a room with coloured light. Colour is then changed slowly, creating at times a sense of drifting and dizziness.

The effect of coloured light on humans hasn't been fully explored. There is some scientific research, none of which is proven enough to be mentioned. It is,

Figure 4.26 James Turrell's coloured light installation changes perception of space in the VW Museum. (Photo: Florian Holzherr)

Figure 4.27 Supersaturation: an orange T5 fluorescent heightens the perception of the orange shelf, SJ Berwin HQ. (Photo: Andy Spain)

desks and on selected architectural elements, contributes significantly when branding a space. The effect of coloured light can be intensified when used in combination with same coloured surfaces. 'Lighting supersaturation' heightens the saturation of a coloured surface. It generates a visual richness otherwise not achievable with coloured light only.

The corporate scheme is often restricted to a single brand colour.

A light installation or a nightclub scheme allows for an unlimited use of coloured dynamic light. Here the colour change, rhythm and sequencing can be explored to the limit. When used in an architectural context, coloured light helps to limit the scheme to a few chosen colours. Mimicking nature's colours can be of great help on many occasions. A popular example is the dark blue colour resembling the evening sky and a sunset orange. The harmonious warm/cold contrast and the choice of a complementary colour scheme ever-present in nature work well together.

Within a colour wheel, the complementary colours can be found opposite to each other and are perceived as contrasting. Green and red are complementary partners and signal colours at the same time. They compete for attention when covering spaces in equal doses. In nature, however, colours usually don't show up in equal quantity. The dense green of a jungle is interrupted and enriched by bright red or yellow blossom spots. The same applies in a lighting scheme where, for example, a subtle base blue colour laid out allows the brighter complementary orange colours to set accents only. The bright colours enhance the elements within the space while the base colour sets the ambience. Whilst complementary colours are perceived as vibrant, energetic and overwhelming, analogous colours are more balanced and lack contrast. Analogous colours sit beside each other on the colour wheel and are harmonious and subtle. These schemes need also one colour setting the ambience or background while the second colour accentuates. The third colour is left to assist one or both of the first two colours.

however, apparent that coloured light affects our mood when used to these extremes. Dyeing a room or parts of it in coloured light, or using it as a sole light source, requires therefore special attention and care. When used in public spaces, as in hospitals, it certainly has to involve research and testing prior to consideration.

There are two questions one should ask when designing with coloured light: 'Why am I using coloured light?' and: 'Why am I using this specific colour?' If one can't answer the two questions above convincingly there is probably no need to use coloured light at all.

A strong argument that answers both these questions is to use coloured light when designing for a corporation. Companies use colour to distinguish themselves from their competitors. Using light in a company brand colour, i.e. behind logos, reception

Figure 4.28 Complementing colours used on this lighting scheme by Speirs and Major.

Whether the colour scheme is complementary, analogous, triadic, split complementary or tetradic, the right quantity of each colour is necessary to create a well-balanced lighting scheme. This implies that once colours are chosen, one is left to experiment and play with the colour to get the right colour mixture.

Colour wheel schemes can help to narrow down the endless choices of colour combination. They are not general rules that must be obeyed, however. Colour has always been subject of personal preference and can therefore be used to ones own taste, providing the two questions mentioned previously have been answered in favour of the project.

Complementary contrast

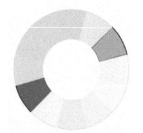

Analogous colour

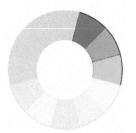

Triadic colour scheme

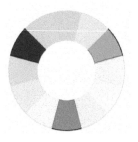

Figure 4.29 Colour schemes visualized on a colour wheel.

DO I NEED A DYNAMIC LIGHTING SCHEME, USING A CIRCADIAN RHYTHM?

As mentioned in Chapter 1, light can emit in various whites. A dynamic lighting scheme allows one to change the colour temperature of the white light between warm white, neutral white and cold white. The change can happen throughout a day, gradually and imperceptibly, or more suddenly in a more spectacular manner. Dynamic lighting allows one to change the feel of a space at the press of a button.

There are several pitfalls and benefits of dynamic lighting that need to be considered. Dynamic schemes often serve another, less spectacular purpose.

Does it feel natural?

In most cases, the white light in a dynamic scheme should feel natural. An observer looking at a weak light source emitting cold white light perceives it as unnatural. A person exposed to low-level cold light experiences the light as uncomfortable. Colour temperature is closely linked to the amount of light. Kruithof's chart shows the relationship of light level to colour temperature and the area that we perceive as pleasing. It follows the observations we make throughout a typical sunny day. We experience the warm evening light of the setting sun in lower light levels. The midday sun, on the other hand, creates a high light level combined with cold white light. We seem to instinctively prefer what nature presents to us daily.

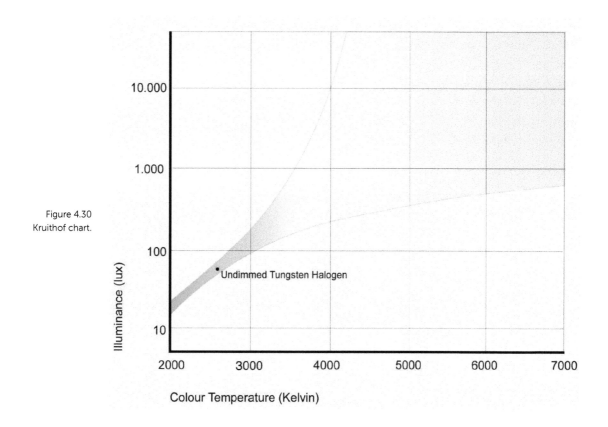

Figure 4.30
Kruithof chart.

Figure 4.31 Light colour temperature throughout a day. (Picture: Planlicht Lighting)

Circadian rhythm

Natural light and its intensity are important as they not only influence our preference for artificial light temperature, they also set our inner clock. This inner clock is called the circadian rhythm and it manages our body's daily patterns. It releases melatonin in the evening, making us sleepy, and frees testosterone in the morning, waking us up. Light, or the absence of light, sets this inner clock. People not exposed to natural daylight profit from the introduction of dynamic light mimicking the light colour throughout the day. Dynamic light allows the body to follow its natural rhythm and therefore makes us more productive.

What light colour?

A highly energetic cold bluish morning light, for example, causes our bodies to wake up. Knowing that a morning boost of light is needed should influence the design of breakfast lounges in hotels, metro stations and our work environment. It can even help to suppress jet-lag by stimulating the body to produce testosterone, thereby resetting the inner body clock.

Neutral white dominates throughout midday and the afternoon, keeping the body awake and alert, whereas the white light in the evening contains red light, making it appear warm. This warm white is what we crave in the evening when reading a book or when we have our dinner.

In summary – a typical dynamic lighting sequence mimicking daylight is to be in the morning a highly

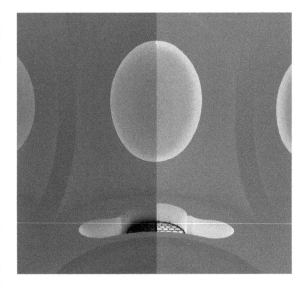

Figure 4.32 Colour temperature of the light within the building changes from 2700K in the morning to 4000 during midday returning to 2700K in the evening St. Moritz Church, Augsburg.

energetic, bluish white. This light changes throughout the midday into a neutral white to turn in the evenings into a relaxing warm white. The intensity changes and colour temperature have to be guided by Kruithof's chart.

DO I NEED A THREE-POINT LIGHT APPROACH FOR A SPEAKER?

The three-point light approach is used to illuminate and shape three-dimensional objects and people. The three light sources are positioned to throw pleasant light onto a person or object, giving volume and a balanced appearance but no drama. Photographers and camera operators use three-point lighting predominately for portrait scenes.

The main or key light source is positioned in front of the subject at a forty-five-degree angle. It provides most of the light needed and will produce dramatic contrasting light and shadows. The effect can be softened by using a more diffused light source but it will still leave one part of the subject in relative darkness. A fill light can help here to fill the dark areas with light as it is positioned opposite the key light. It is not as intense as the key light but it lifts and defines the neglected parts of the subject. Both lights help to define and model the front of the subject, creating a balanced front lighting. The subject, however, still appears to merge with the background. To prevent this from happening, a light aiming at the back of the person is introduced. The backlight separates the subject from the background and creates a rim light, making the subject appear more three-dimensional.

Instead of using a direct backlight one can illuminate the background. If this is brightly lit, a direct backlight is not necessary.

This lighting technique used in portrait photography can be transferred into architectural lighting design. It is best applied when people speaking in public need to be lit appropriately from a distance. When speeches are photographed, televised or streamed, the three-point lighting should create

Figure 4.33 All three light sources are diffused to soften the light. The key light is on 100% intensity, the fill light is significantly lower (40–60%) while the backlight needs to provide only 10–20%.

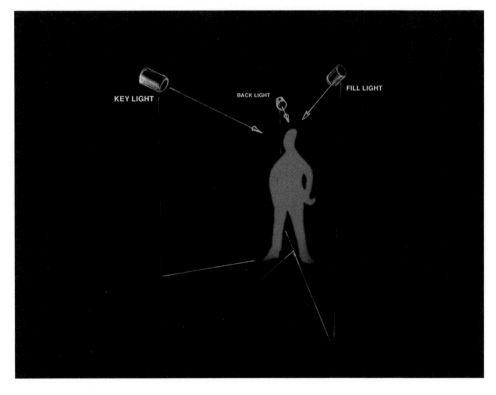

balanced lighting and a vertical illuminance of over 500 lux. This will generally ensure good light quality and good light levels for the recording devices.

This approach can usually be observed in public buildings where speeches are held and sometimes recorded. It applies, for example, to priests doing a mass in a church as much as to parliamentarians holding a speech or professors giving a lecture.

The principles are always the same: two front lights to secure a good illumination of the visible and a backlight separating the subject from the background. If the ceiling is too low to provide glare-free shielded light at the right angle, one can consider diffused linear or panel lighting instead. A single diffused light source mimics the overcast sky and is able to supply the desired light quality and light level.

Figure 4.34 Doris Day lit by a key-, fill- and backlight, doctormacro.com.

Figure 4.35 The lighting of the Great Room in the Royal Society of Arts Head Quarter. The key- and fill light are supplied from the left and the right top ledge. Back light is coming directly from above. (Arch: Matthew Lloyd Architects; Photo: Andy Spain)

Figure 4.36 HSBC video conference and meeting room. Rectangular pendant supplies the vertical light level needed. Illuminated wall divider and spotlights provide back lighting.

DO I NEED TO ILLUMINATE STATUES AND OBJECTS?

The lighting to a statue is part of an architectural entity and therefore has to reflect the context into which it is placed. The surrounding is as important as the position, form, colour and texture of the statue. Is the statue an integrated part of the building or does it stand apart? Is it the only statue or is it one of many? If it's the latter, what is its hierarchy? Where can the light be positioned and where are the power access points? Once these questions are answered the lighting can take place.

What applies to people can be applied to objects and statues when it comes to lighting. A statue gets a good illumination when the three-point rule is applied. However, statue lighting tends to be more dramatic and often fill light is very subtle or not used at all. The angles often vary as this helps to create a more dramatic effect. Due to the geometry of a space or power access restrictions three-point lighting is rarely used when illuminating statues outside of museums. Lighting a sculpture outside a museum can involve the architecture it surrounds and allows one to set a scene for a sculpture if necessary.

When three-point lighting is applied, either light quantity or the angles of the luminaires are used in an unusual way. In addition, the light contrast is emphasized and only parts of the statue are lit. One can choose what part of the statue deserves emphasis and what effect one wants to create. If the strong facial expression of a statue has to be highlighted then only this part gets illuminated while the other areas remain in the dark. This draws the eye of the spectator to desired areas only.

Strong light contrast has been used in many film noir movies but also in horror movies. A single narrow light from the side or below, leaving elements

Figure 4.37 St Moritz Church. Key and fill light are illuminating the 2-metre Christ statue from the front. The backlight is supplied by the lit wall. The unusually strong backlight illuminates the entire 15m wall and brings the statue forwards.

Figure 4.38 Main light provided by two lights from above, grounding the statue. Three floor recessed uplights are highlighting the nose and the wings of the *Grain of Rice* sculpture from BASED UPON, for HSBC Hong Kong.

of a person to merge with the darkness, are probably the strongest effects lighting can achieve. This can be emphasized by colour, light pattern and light intensity. This light effect is powerful and rarely used in interior contexts, more often when lighting statues in landscapes.

DO I NEED TO ILLUMINATE A PICTURE?

To light a wall-mounted picture is not always necessary as the ambient light in a space might be sufficient. This lighting approach or philosophy of letting the artwork be without any further accentuation has gained more and more acceptance in modern galleries. Lighting designers create a uniform light resembling an overcast sky to illuminate the artworks and the walls equally. This approach creates a bright and open atmosphere, inviting all to enter and to stroll through a space. A similar effect is achieved when washing the wall with light. All items displayed on the wall are lit evenly; there is no accentuation, contrast or drama. Another effect is created with spotlights focused on the artwork only. This contrast-filled lighting approach creates a strong focus on each picture separately. It further creates a more private space around the artwork for the observer.

For both approaches, the quality of light is very important. The position of the light has to be chosen carefully so as not to interfere with observation. Shadows caused by the observer or reflection from the light source must be avoided. Light scallops occur often when directed light hits the wall.

Figure 4.39 Left: the art work lit precisely looks more appealing. Right: light scallops on the wall should be avoided or softened if possible.

Their shape and the sudden contrast of the light detracts from the artwork. If possible, they should be avoided; if not, they should at least be softened using softening lenses. The light has to cover the entire picture and softly lose intensity as it moves away from the picture. Spotlights with framers allow one to treat the artwork exclusively, leaving the wall in relative darkness. There is no light around the picture to introduce it. The sudden light/dark contrast makes the picture stand out.

Not only the way light is delivered but also the properties of the light are of importance. The colour rendition should be CRI 98 and higher. The chosen colour temperature must support the artwork.

Most importantly, if light-sensitive artwork is

Figure 4.40 Warm high CRI light is illuminating this mural. The light on the floor separates the picture visually from the floor.

exhibited, the light level should not exceed the lux level allowed as this might destroy the artwork. When still using a halogen light source an infrared filter is essential as these light waves are damaging to a lot of artwork.

HOW DO I CONTROL GLARE?

We have probably all experienced discomforting or disabling glare. The most extreme case is probably the main-beam of an approaching car in the night. The bright gathered light shines directly into the eyes while the overall surroundings are dark.

Glare can be defined as bright light that impairs the vision of a person. One can differentiate between discomforting glare and disabling glare. There are two factors that affect how glare is perceived.

1. Ratio: the disruptive light is significantly brighter than the surrounding light within the direct field of vision.
2. Angle: the direct or reflected light is angled, pointing straight into a person's direct field of vision.

Glare is perceived as discomforting if the angle of the light is steep and the light ratio is high. Discomforting glare can quickly turn into disabling glare if the angle

Figure 4.41 Left: glare caused by strong directional point light in a dark ambient. Right: diffused panel light creating a lighter ambient causing no glare.

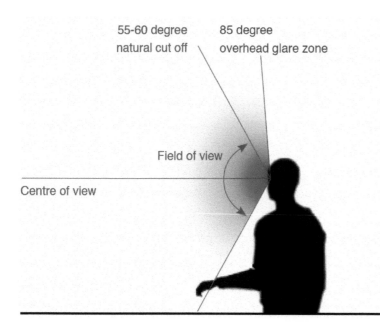

Figure 4.42 Luminaires within the red field of view can cause glare. The closer they are to the centre of view, the more obtrusive they are.

of the light is close to the centre of the view while the surrounding area is in relative darkness. This is why the headlights of cars are perceived as disabling. The same applies to interior lighting. Light sources should ideally be kept out of the field of view.

If they are within the field of view of 120 degrees they should not be pointing towards the field of view. Recessing the luminaire or using louvres can help to reduce glare.

Glare can be calculated and compared with a Unified Glare Rating figure (UGR). The higher the UGR is the less tolerable the glare. The ideal UGR is different for each space within a building. The glare/UGR value in offices and laboratories has to be low. Someone sitting steadily over a long period of time, looking into one direction only, can tolerate less glare than a person who moves around in corridors or shops and who sees a constantly changing scene. For an office environment glare figures below and around a UGR 15 are acceptable while a Unified Glare Rating of UGR 30 is perceived as intolerable.

What applies to direct glare also applies to reflective glare. The position of the luminaire and the contrast define the reflective glare intensity.

The right position of the luminaire is hard to define. The law of reflection states that light hitting

Here some UGR recommendations for working environments.

Working area/ type of work	Maximum allowed UGR
Drawing rooms	16
Offices	19
Industrial work, fine	22
Industrial work, medium	25
Industrial work, coarse	28

a surface at an incoming angle Θ will be reflected at the same angle Θ. This rule applied to the light leaving the luminaire helps to confirm whether the light fixture will cause glare.

Consider that reflective light is not only important in an office but also in galleries and shops. Here one wants to make sure that the picture or the product is visible without any disruptions. The luminaires have to be placed to avoid direct and indirect glare. To position them rightly one must consider the position of the person within the space. Of particular interest are the main viewpoints the person experiences in a resting position.

Figure 4.43 Light reflected on a surface. Incident ray angle = reflected ray angle.

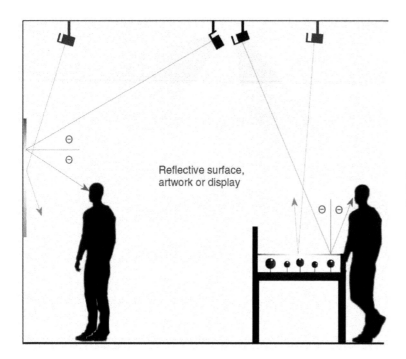

Figure 4.44 Typical viewpoints of a person in a shop or gallery. The green luminaires don't cause glare while the black ones do.

Reflective surface, artwork or display

HOW DO I CREATE LAYERS OF LIGHT?

Using only a single light source or light layer can make a room appear bland and the light uncomfortable. Introducing various light layers into a scheme helps one to avoid discomforting shadowing and create a well-balanced lighting scheme. Lighting designers distinguish between three types of lighting. They are separated by function and position, and are called task, ambient and accent light. When used together in the right combination they help to create depth and a visually interesting space.

Task light

Task light, as the name reveals, helps us to perform tasks such as reading, writing, assembling, dining, cooking, operating, etc. The typical minimal light level of task lights begins with 300 lux and can go up to 100,000 lux in operating cavities. Whether one is reading or performing an operation, the contrast between task and surrounding light must be kept low, to avoid constant adaptation of the eye, which can be tiring.

The easiest way to deliver task light is to bring it physically to the user. In this case, one uses desktop luminaires, floor-standing fixtures or pendant

Figure 4.45 Most tasks are performed at a certain height. This is where the lighting has to work.

luminaires. Their flexibility and design allows one to deliver the right type of light, free of glare and shadow. They are usually separately controllable and can be turned on and dimmed to the ideal light level when necessary. The other way to deliver task light is via track lights, or surface-mounted or down-lights. They deliver a task light either to a small area only or, in an open-plan office, for example, over a larger area.

General/ambient light

General or ambient light provides an entire space with a basic light level. The space is lit to allow one to move safely around. The light level can be lower than with a task light. The light distribution is more even and perceived as comfortable. Any luminaire types that are capable of providing a space with a basic and even light level are suitable. This can mean down-lights, up-lighters, movable luminaires or pendants. Luminaires with wide-beam angles, luminaires with diffused light sources, chandeliers or indirect up-lighters allow one to use lesser light sources and generate a good ambient light. Ambient light is essential in a lighting scheme. Once it is laid out, it serves as a base and one can start adding more layers of light to the lighting scheme. Missing task or accent light can be added to enhance the space further with light.

Accent light

Accent light serves to highlight an area or an object within a room. This can range from an entire textured wall that deserves to be highlighted to paintings, sculptures and architectural elements.

This light is more focused and more intense, creating drama and making the lit object a visual point of interest. To achieve this, the light contrast needs to be high. The accent light level should be three to five times higher than the general light level surrounding it. A spartan space doesn't require a lot of light contrast whereas a space where a lot is happening needs more light punch to increase visual focus.

In many cases, the reflected light from the accent light is sufficient to serve as general light. Two good examples are a lit feature wall in a corridor and lit paintings in a gallery. In both cases, the reflected light creates sufficient light to move safely around and no additional lighting needs to be added.

Figure 4.46 Ambient light has to work on the floor surface and allows safe moving through the space.

Figure 4.47 Accent light has to work horizontally and vertically and on all levels – everywhere where there is a point of interest worth accentuating.

Figure 4.48 The luminaires highlighting the art work in this exhibition produce sufficient spill light for the general light. There is no need for additional illumination. (Arch: Theis and Khan; Lighting: Mindseye)

Typical light sources for accent light are punchy luminaires with a narrow light-beam distribution. Amongst others, recessed up-/down-lights, track lights, picture lights or cove lights can be used, providing they are powerful enough to create the light contrast needed. Their zone of illumination must be restricted to the area of interest only.

Many interior designers use decorative luminaires to add accent light to a space. In this case the luminaire itself becomes the object of interest emitting its own light.

The number of lighting layers used is dependent on the complexity of the space. A task-light treatment can add enough light to the space to serve as general light. In this case, one layer is sufficient.

More complex spaces, however, rely heavily on multiple layers. These are necessary to light and emphasize all elements within the space.

Figure 4.49 (a) General light, provided by uplight; (b) Accent light, washing the walls; (c) Task light over the table.

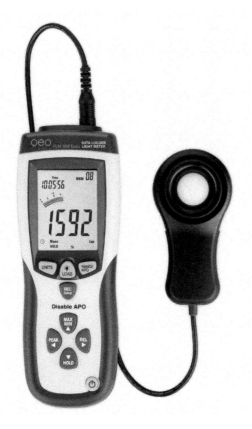

Figure 4.50 A lux meter with a measurements surface covered by a white opal dome.

Light level in Nature	
0.0001 lux	Moonless, overcast night sky
0.27–1.0 lux	Full moon on a clear night
100 lux	Very dark overcast day
400 lux	Sunrise or sunset on a clear day
1000 lux	Overcast day
10000–25000 lux	Full daylight - not direct sun
30000–100000lux	Direct sunlight

CIBSE Recomendations	
100 lux	Corridors, lifts
150 lux	Restrooms
200 lux	Canteens
300-500 lux	Office
500-1000 lux	Spot welding
1000 lux	Superstore
1000 lux	TV studio

Figure 4.51 Lux level chart.

WHAT LUX LEVEL DO I NEED?

When coming up with a lighting design for a space, one question will always occur: 'Have I allowed for enough light?' The feasibility of a lighting-design scheme depends also on whether the expected light levels in a space are achievable. All the lamps introduced into a scheme will differ in light quality and intensity. They still have one thing in common, however, which is that they emit a certain amount of light into a space. That light intensity can be measured with a lux meter. A lux meter measures the lumens or all light falling onto its measuring surface.

The lumen value on that small surface is extrapolated to $1m^2$ ($10.8ft^2$). This is necessary because lux is defined in lumens per square metre.

$$1 \text{ lux} = 1\text{lm per m}^2$$

To see things in perspective when aiming at light level, consider that direct sunlight generates around 70,000 lumens per square metre – this is 70,000 lux, while on a moonless overcast night there are only 0.001 lux.

We need to be able to measure the amount of light on a surface to establish whether the light level is sufficient for the task we need to perform. For example, walking requires less light than reading. The British Chartered Institution of Building Services Engineers (CIBSE) has released recommendations of lux level for various tasks and environments.

When selecting lamps, one has to bear in mind the light levels that are required for the areas illuminated.

The higher the lumen output of the lamp the better. Lamps with a reflector are generating more lux on a surface than lamps without a reflector and the same lumen output. To give an example, a LED lamp with a reflector emitting 800lm gives good reading light. To achieve an equivalent light level with a multidirectional lamp, one requires more than the 3300lm of a 35w fluorescent lamp, or equivalent multidirectional LED replacement.

luminance (cd/m²)

0.0   500.0   1500.0   2250.0

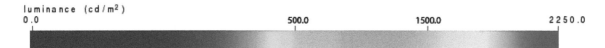

Figure 4.52 Example of a light calculation.

One should also remember that with age our visual perception changes. As we grow older we lose the ability to see as clearly and need more light to perform tasks. One must allow for more lux when designing for the elderly.

A lux meter might allow one to provide a light-quantity reading after a project is finished, but in most cases this is too late. The help of a lighting calculation is required.

A lighting calculation can prove that a room is sufficiently lit. There is more on this in the next chapter as it forms part of the deliverables.

Chapter 5

THE SERVICES AND DELIVERABLES

THE PREVIOUS FOUR CHAPTERS HAVE SHOWN that a lighting design depends on technical knowledge but also an understanding of light and its effects. Equally important is the design aspect, which depends heavily on the sensitivity of the lighting designer. The beauty and the challenge of being a lighting designer is that no project or client is the same. In addition to this, every architect or interior designer has a different way of working and presenting their work. This means that every lighting concept received will look different as it should reflect the visual language of the architect's presentation but also their preferences. The other deliverables of the lighting package, however, must be always the same. Lighting design accompanies the process of the construction or renovation of a building. The services that a lighting designer offers are closely linked to the architect's 'Plan of Work'. In the UK, they are typically divided into seven stages defined by the Royal Institute of British Architects (RIBA).

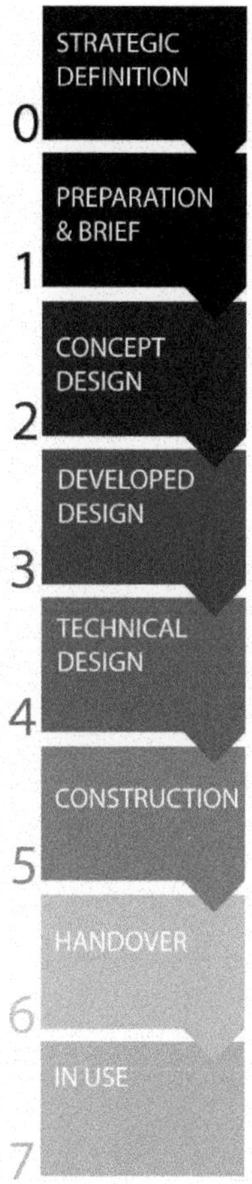

Each of these stages demands deliverables from the architect whether construction drawings, reports or designs. Lighting design consultancies divide their service package into five project phases. They are tailored to cover all aspects of lighting throughout a project. Each phase finishes with the submission of deliverables. This chapter explains the typical phases of a lighting design project and its deliverables.

Figure 5.01 The eight stages of RIBA's 'Plan of Work'.

THE FIVE PROJECT PHASES

1. Orientation or concept phase (broadly in line with the RIBA Stage 2)

The first phase after having received a brief is the orientation or concept phase. This phase covers first meetings or workshops with the architects and clients. It serves to define general design principles within a project. Eventually, it all leads to a creation of a concept document. The creation of a concept document is very time-intensive. To avoid having to re-do the concept document if it does not match the expectations of the architects, a pre-concept is recommended. This rough sketch concept shows the main treatments and ideas of the lighting design. The document forms the base of a workshop with the architect. After the workshop, the main lighting strategy is clear, and one can embed the comments and changes into the concept document. This concept document represents the joint lighting approach. The architect stands behind the document when it is presented to the client. The changes afterwards are minimal and can be implemented in the next phase.

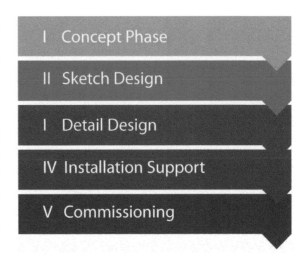

Figure 5.02 Typical services package provided by lighting design consultancies.

2. Sketch design and specification of lighting equipment (broadly in line with the RIBA Stage 3)

The lighting package produced in this phase is based on the drawings that are created by the architect in the design development phase. At this point, many aspects of the architect's design are not set yet and are therefore likely to change. This means that it is highly likely that the lighting design will change. This phase requires the production of a full first lighting package. It includes specification of the luminaires and the load schedule, including the lighting layout and detail drawings. The lighting package is fairly accurate and can be priced while the design can be evaluated and embedded into all documentation.

3. Detail design and specification of lighting equipment (broadly in line with the RIBA Stage 4)

All changes of the architect's revised and final drawings package will have to be considered here. It is most likely that all documents will need to be changed to reflect the altered design. By this time, the pricing of the luminaire package is known. This stage allows one to correct the design and to reduce the cost if

necessary by changing the specification and detail of the luminaires. At the end stands a final design package that includes the final calculations, lighting layout, detail design, detail drawings, load schedule and specification.

4. Installation support phase (broadly in line with the RIBA Stage 5)

This phase, as the name suggests, allows one to offer support during construction and installation of a project. The support can be offered in response to RFI (Requests For Information). RFI are issued if the installer has questions regarding the order, installation and setting out of the luminaires. In some cases, RFI lead to changing the lighting information to accommodate new circumstances on site. This phase should allow for site visits and meeting with all parties involved.

5. Commissioning and focusing (broadly in line with the RIBA Stage 6)

Commissioning is important as it allows one to define the various light levels of each scene. This happens together with the engineer of the company that provided the control system. It requires a pre-visit report in form of a scene-setting document.

The lighting designer continues to be on site to make sure that the luminaires are positioned correctly and to establish the quality of the install. The installation ends with a report of the installation listing changes that might have to take place.

YOUR DELIVERABLES

The deliverables on a project might differ depending on the involvement of the lighting consultants. The following items are the standard deliverables that form part of the work of a lighting designer. All the listed documents communicate and confirm the design intended. While the form can vary, the main message has to be clear for all parties.

Concept document

The concept document explains the lighting design to the client. A project can have more than one client. There may be the client or the investor covering projects costs and there may be the architect, who is the party that often selects the lighting designer. Concept documents have to communicate to both parties. The architect is capable of imagining how light within a space will work through his or her education and experience. Many paying clients and investors need a concept that shows in detail what the desired lighting treatment and the effect of the light is.

The main communication tool is reference imagery showing the desired lighting effects. They explain more than a thousand words would. They are often accompanied by edited 2D or 3D images provided by the architects. These help to show the light effect in the space. In some cases, it is required that the space is drawn and the light rendered in by hand.

Figure 5.03 Two very different concept documents. A: the minimal hand-rendered St Moritz Church concept for John Pawson Architects.

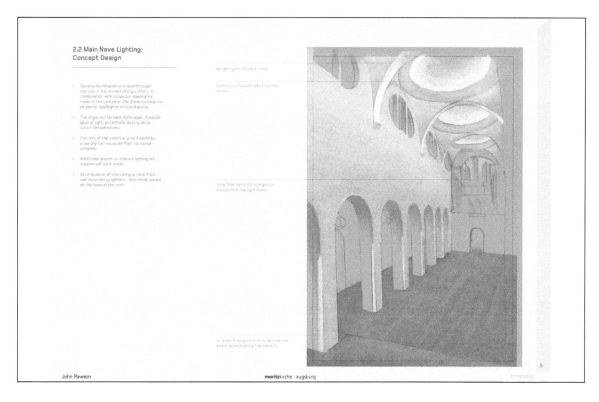

Figure 5.04 Two very different concept documents. B: the expressive concept document for Virgile and Partners includes reference images.

Photoshop, Illustrator and InDesign are the main tools for helping clients to visualize the lighting effects on a project. The more drawings and renderings available the better the lighting effect can be demonstrated. Text allows one to add more information and round the presentation document up. The less text the better – if text is used, one should either keep it brief or use bullet points. Presentation documents can contain up to fifty pages; therefore, one should restrict the text to the necessary, and the document should be as structured, short and interesting as possible.

Lighting calculations

It is not rare for a lighting calculation to be necessary during the actual concept phase. A quick lighting calculation can confirm whether a light treatment is feasible in extreme conditions, for example, areas where lighting from very high points is intended or one will be relying on reflected light. A lighting calculation can confirm that the desired treatment can achieve the necessary light level and can be included in the concept document.

Once the concept document is approved, lighting calculations are often necessary in more detail. Certain areas require specific light levels and uniformity levels. These levels are defined in the UK by the CIBSE Lighting Guide and can vary from 100 lux in a corridor to 1,000 lux in a supermarket.

Calculations can give a pretty accurate prediction of light level on all horizontal and vertical planes within a space. The more precise the definition of the space is, the more accurate the calculation is. Ascertaining the reflectance of the walls is crucial. One wants to know what material and colour the wall is as this allows one to set the reflectance. Big furniture should be included in the 3D model as this also helps one to get a more accurate calculation.

The choice of the luminaire is the next important step. Many producers have photometric files and place them on their web pages for download.

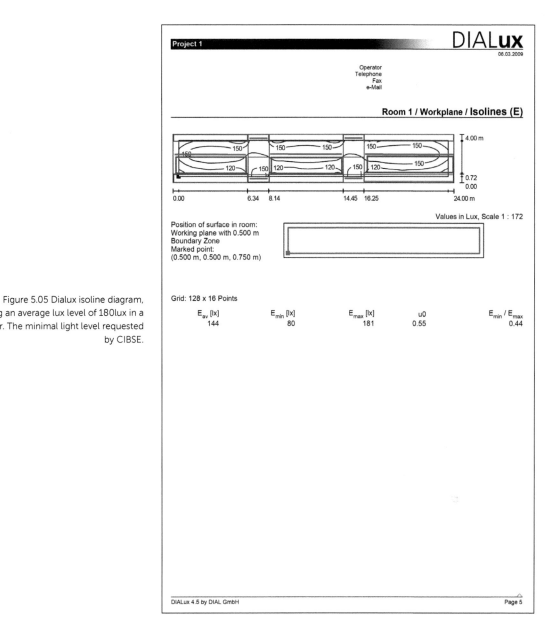

DIALux
06.03.2009

Operator
Telephone
Fax
e-Mail

Room 1 / Workplane / Isolines (E)

Values in Lux, Scale 1 : 172

Position of surface in room:
Working plane with 0.500 m
Boundary Zone
Marked point:
(0.500 m, 0.500 m, 0.750 m)

Grid: 128 x 16 Points

E_{av} [lx]	E_{min} [lx]	E_{max} [lx]	u0	E_{min} / E_{max}
144	80	181	0.55	0.44

DIALux 4.5 by DIAL GmbH

Page 5

Figure 5.05 Dialux isoline diagram, showing an average lux level of 180lux in a corridor. The minimal light level requested by CIBSE.

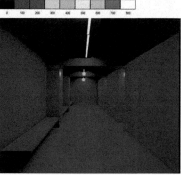

Figure 5.06 A rendering and a false colour rendering in a corridor lit by artificial light.

luminance (cd/m²)
0.0   500.0   1500.0   2250.0

Figure 5.07 This more accurate false colour rendering shows the daylight analysis of St Moritz Church, Augsburg.

The photometric files have to be imported into the lighting calculation programme. The most common lighting calculation programs are the freeware Dialux, Relux and Radiance. Various plug-ins for major architectural 3D software are also available. Some of them are capable of accurate photorealistic rendering, which is interesting for the client. The lighting designer is more interested in the photometric values they produce. The false colour image and the isoline diagram probably show the light level most clearly.

Other outputs of the calculations reveal information on the average lux level, uniformity, glare and the wattage per square metre. This information can determine whether a lighting design scheme works or simply whether a luminaire is fit for purpose.

Emergency lighting

Residential projects usually don't require emergency lighting calculations but in any commercial and public building one has to make sure that the light level in an emergency does comply with the CIBSE's Emergency Lighting Regulations. Lighting calculation programs allow scene setting, so one can use these to perform an emergency lighting calculation if necessary.

Testing luminaires

Lighting calculations are a good way of predicting average values and getting specific numbers. What they are not able to do is to show us how a luminaire performs in reality. A calculation cannot replace the human eye and human judgement. Which luminaire to use in a detail can often be determined by a mock-up only. This involves ordering various luminaires from different manufacturers with similar specifications and testing them against each other. The quality of a luminaire and, more importantly, the quality of the light are best evaluated by testing them in-house. Sales representatives of lighting manufacturers play an important part. They help to source the chosen fixture and can provide one with all relevant information. Good sales representatives are visiting lighting design consultancies on a regular basis, updating them on the latest luminaire ranges.

Specification

Once a luminaire has been approved by a lighting calculation, a lighting test and the lighting designer, it has to be included in a specification sheet. The sheet forms part of the specification document and includes all the relevant information about a luminaire. The information contains images, order numbers and other additional information that allow the general contractor to order the exact fixtures and all accessories necessary. The more information that is included, the less likely it is that errors will occur.

The specification has to include the contact details of the manufacturer's sales representative, the project name and a project number. Throughout the process of the design, sales representatives are involved in obtaining the samples and information on the luminaire or the first rough budget pricing. By the time the specification has been decided, they can have a good understanding of the project and the role of their luminaire. It is not unusual that one gets a call from the sales representative trying to either confirm a specification or making one aware of fixtures ordered that are not complying with the specification sheet.

Incorrect fixtures arriving on site mean that a new order has to be placed, which can delay a project significantly. Sales representatives can help to protect a specification.

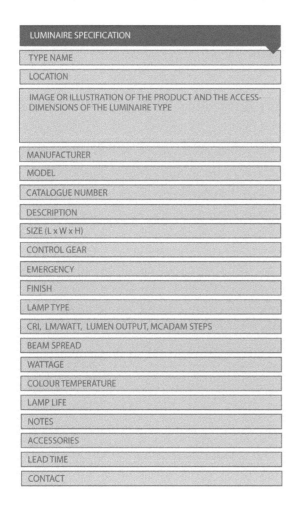

Figure 5.08 Specification sheets can vary significantly depending on country or even between lighting consultancies. The list shows the minimal requirements for a luminaire specification.

Lighting layout

The specification of the luminaire will determine the number and position of the luminaires within a lighting layout. A lighting layout is a CAD drawing showing the position of the luminaires on the reflected ceiling plan provided by the architect. This gives the contractor a precise position of the luminaires within a building. It also includes the circuit numbers and the control group the luminaires form.

Depending on the complexity of the lighting design, the lighting layout might be split into a high-, mid- and a low-level layout. The low-level plan shows the position of the luminaires in or close to the ground. The mid-level shows luminaires that are wall-mounted or integrated into furniture, while the high-level plan shows the luminaires mounted into or close to the ceiling.

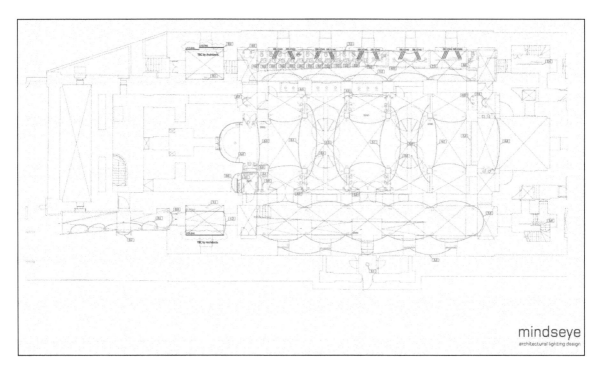

Figure 5.09 Typical lighting layout showing in plan-view the position of the luminaires on the high-level.

Detail drawing

While the lighting layout shows the position of the luminaires within the space, the indicative detail drawing shows their exact position within a lighting detail. If, for example, the luminaires are part of a ceiling raft, a detailed drawing of the raft edge and the exact position of the luminaires will form part of the detail drawing. A detail drawing can show the manufacturer's standard detail for a luminaire. It can also be the result of a bespoke detail that has been mocked up and tested.

Figure 5.10 Typical detail drawings showing the luminaire in its surrounding, the method of attachment and relevant measurements.

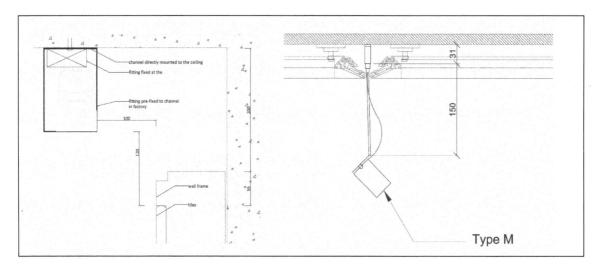

Final detail drawings should not leave the office unless they have been confirmed by either the manufacturer or a mock-up.

When lighting designers are involved early enough in a project, it will allow them to determine the ideal dimensions of a detail. The drawing dimensions are taken on by the architect and included in their drawing set. Often the detail dimensions are 'negotiated' with the architect. There is the ideal lighting detail of the lighting designer and the ideal ceiling height that an architect has in mind. If the desired space is not available and one has agreed on a new dimension, the detail and probably the specification will have to be changed to achieve the desired effect.

Lighting designers' detail drawings do not serve as construction drawings. Once the new detail drawing is set it serves as an indicative template for the architect, interior designer or contractor.

Calculations

Detail drawings are also used to define the luminaires, check their quantity and their exact position. These drawings are not part of the deliverables but rather a layer within the detail drawings. The layer can be removed later but is substantial in the Stage 2 sketch phase as much as in the Stage 3 detail phase.

Checking whether a beam angle is feasible for a space but also whether one has allowed for suffficient light sources is very simple in lighting design software. Establishing whether there are enough spotlights or whether one can cover an area needed is equally easy with the beam-angle method in a CAD program.

BEAM-SPOT DEFINITION FOR A TABLE

Let's say one is working in a CAD software, laying out the luminaires, and is trying to establish the quantity of down- or spotlights needed to cover a specific area. The designer does not know what luminaire type he or she will be specifying but wants to know where and how many luminaires should be placed. Depending on the effect one is looking to achieve the beam angle will vary. For example, perhaps one is trying to cover a narrow display table with light.

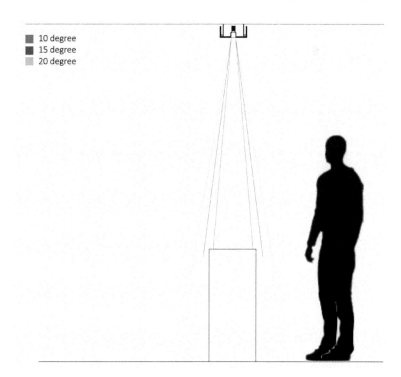

■ 10 degree
■ 15 degree
  20 degree

Figure 5.11 Side view – showing three various beam angles on a table.

Figure 5.12 Top view – showing the light on the table.

An elevation with the table width and length, including the room height, is required. One then checks the available beam angle of various lighting suppliers and draws the selected beam angles on the elevation. The beam angle lines touching the surface define the diameter of the luminaire. That diameter can then be drawn and is placed onto the plan view.

In this case, the ten-degree beam angle drawn in orange is the right beam angle for a down-light or spotlight placed above the display table. This way we can make sure that light really hits the table only, creating a focus onto the table and not spilling light onto the floor.

BEAM-SPOT DEFINITION AND QUANTITY FOR A SPACE

A similar approach can be used to establish luminaire angle and quantity for an entire room. Let's say it is only possible to use lights in the middle of a room because the rest of the ceiling has to be kept clean. The same method of working on the section first, then the plan view, must be applied. The section of the space is drawn and the light beam is angled to cover

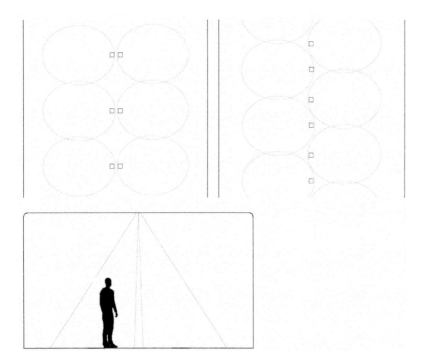

Figure 5.13 Section and plan view of a space. The drawing allows checking the quantity and beam angle of luminaires within space. 30 degree spotlights are tilted by 20 degrees. This allows a pairing or aligning of spotlights rather than using a grid.

the space. The former round-beam spot becomes an oval and covers more surface in one direction.

This method allows one to use fewer down-lights in a space. One must be careful about the possibility of glare in a room with low ceilings or if the lights are tilted too much.

BEAM-SPOT CHECK FOR OBJECTS

This CAD method is crucial for defining the position of an adjustable down-light. Whether an adjustable will hit its target and what angle is needed can be established with a quick CAD drawing exercise. This is not as important for a track-mounted spotlight as this allows almost free movement in all directions. But if the light is ceiling-recessed and the tilt angle is limited, it is important to test whether the light reaches its target before drilling the hole into a ceiling.

A section of the space is required. If it is not available, one can quickly draw the section by putting the ceiling, wall and floor lines in. Their distance is defined by the ceiling height. The next thing to be sketched is the target; in our case it is a picture.

As a final step, one can mark the beam angle of the specified light in the maximal tilting position on the CAD drawing. If it hits the target, well done; if not, one has to move the beam of light until it hits the target or use a bigger beam angle.

VISIBILITY CHECK

As mentioned previously, good lighting design isn't noticed. One enters a space and it all feels right. Many good lighting schemes depend on details where the light source is not visible. Whether a light is visible can be checked by mocking up the detail. In a complex project, however, not all areas can be mocked up. A visibility check via CAD can help here. The best method is to use the drawing of the lighting detail and put it in its envisaged position. A person of average height is then positioned in the typical and least favourable position in the space. Lines are drawn leaving the eyes of that person towards the luminaire. If the lines hit the luminaire this means that the luminaire is visible and must either be moved or shielded. The same drawing set-up can be used

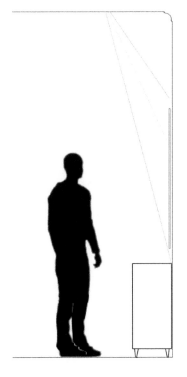

Figure 5.14 Drawings allows establishing the position of the luminaire to the object and the beam angle. Luminaire specified allows for a maximal tilting of 25 degrees. Beam angle of light is 20 degrees.

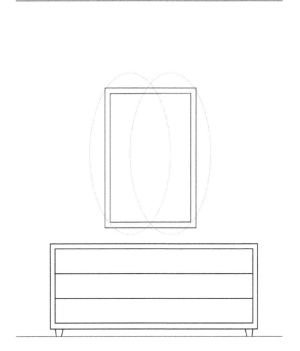

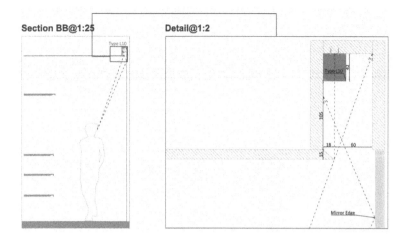

Section BB@1:25   Detail@1:2

Type L10

Type L10

Mirror Edge

Figure 5.15 A person standing in front of a mirrored wall will not see the luminaires. The mirror stops short to avoid visibility of the luminaire. The drawings check the sight line of a person standing at the closest possible point to the mirror.

to verify whether the reflection of the light is visible by the person in a space. A reflection test drawing is more complex as one has to include a reflection surface. The sight line from the person travels towards the reflecting surface and bounces off the material. If the light beam hits the luminaire it means that the light source is visible.

All four methods serve to establish beam angle, quantity and position of luminaires within a space but also within a niche, shelf or any other detail. They allow one to play with the position of a light in a defined space but do not define the light output

required. This needs to be established with a lighting design calculation.

Load and control schedule

The load and control schedule is a central document in a lighting design scheme. It lists the number of luminaires, luminaire types and their electrical load in watts. They are arranged by circuit groups and control methods. It further shows the total load of a project.

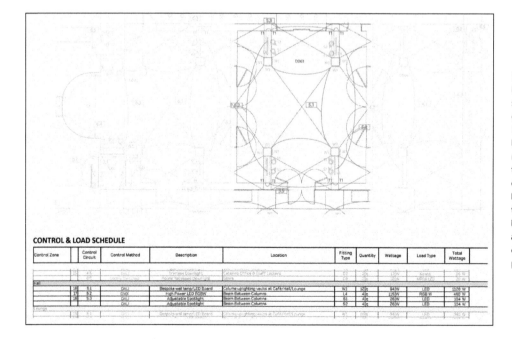

Figure 5.16 The load schedule shows the circuit groups of the hall. Furthermore, it lists the control method, luminaire type, luminaire quantity and the load in Watts they require. The lighting layout above shows the circuit groups position in plan.

CONTROL & LOAD SCHEDULE

Control Zone	Control Circuit	Control Method	Description	Location	Fitting Type	Quantity	Wattage	Load Type	Total Wattage
	4.5	DALI	Trimless Downlight	Catering Office & Staff Lockers	D2	2q	7.3 W	LED	26 W
	5.0	DALI	Trimless Recessed Downlight	Store	D3	1q	20 W	Metal LED	20 W
Hall									
	18	5.1	DALI	Bespoke wall lamp/LED Board	Column uplighting vaults at Café/Hall/Lounge	W3	12q	94 W	LED	1128 W
	17	5.2	DMX	High Power LED RGBW	Beam Between Columns	L4	4q	115 W	RGB W	460 W
	18	5.3	DALI	Adjustable Spotlight	Beam Between Columns	S1	4q	26 W	LED	104 W
			DALI	Adjustable Spotlight	Beam Between Columns	S2	4q	26 W	LED	104 W
Lounge									
		6.1	DALI	Bespoke wall lamp/LED Board	Column uplighting vaults at Café/Hall/Lounge	W3	10q	94 W	LED	940 W

LIGHTING SCENE CHART

						1	2	3	4	5	6	7	8	9	10	11	12	13	14
Control Zone	Control Circuit	Description	Location	Fitting Type		Day As one space	Off As one space	Café & Entrance Evening	Café & Entrance Evening corporate	Café & Entrance Lecture conference	Café & Entrance Concert	Hall Conference Speaker	Hall Projector	Hall Concert	Hall & Lounge Day evening Lecture	Lounge Conference Speaker	Lounge Projector	Lounge Concert	Road
	...88/TL2	Adjustable Spotlight	Beam between Columns	S2		OFF	OFF					60%	OFF	50%	OFF				
		Adjustable Spotlight	Beam between Columns	S2		OFF	OFF					60%	OFF	50%	OFF				
	...88/L3	High Power LED RGBW	Beam between Columns	L4		100%	OFF					95%	40%	100%	50%				
	...88/3L3	Hospoline wall lamp LED board	at Café/Hall/Lounge	W1		100%	Off					50%	5%	5%	50%				

Figure 5.17 The scene chart shows the circuit groups and their status. Depending on the scene and specification of the control gear, they can be set from 0% up to 100% if dimmable. Non-dimmable fixtures are either set to on or off.

The electrical engineer uses this document as it allows one to add the required lighting load to the other expected electrical loads. One can then calculate the incoming load and plan the cabling. The electrician uses it for wiring as it shows the circuit groups and control method. It is further used by the control-system manufacturer in order to quote, provide and assemble the lighting control unit. The general or electrical contractor uses it to order the fixtures as it quantifies and describes the luminaires.

Finally, it serves as the base for the scene-setting document.

Scene-setting document

A scene-chart shows the light level of various scenes. The scenes can either be triggered by pressing a button or by an astronomical clock. Alternatively, a presence detector or a light sensor can activate them. Each scene gets a dedicated row that allows one to set the values for each circuit group.

One should make sure that the values are quoted as perceived brightness. If, for example, the dimming of a luminaire for a particular scene is 30 per cent the perceived intensity of the light is meant and not the actual numerical value of 30 per cent within the dimmer, as they might vary.

The scene-chart serves the lighting-control manufacturer as a reference document to pre-program the scenes before the arrival of the lighting designer. The lighting designer meets in the commissioning period with the lighting-control engineer and goes through each scene, correcting the values to achieve the desired effect. The number of scenes can vary from three scenes in a residential space to up to fifty scenes in a Catholic church. The effect of scene settings is very rewarding and can change the perception of a space dramatically.

Figure 5.18 Corpus Christi Church – three scenes in the main nave. (Arch: Dow Jones; Photo: Julian Adams)

Chapter 6

COMMON PITFALLS

CREATIVITY, SENSITIVITY AND INSTINCT can't be taught – these are left to the reader of this book. The book, however, can set the framework. An important part of the framework is to point out the various mistakes one can make in the process of designing with light. It is important to show the mistakes that can be avoided easily by using the right design detail, method or specification. Some of the pitfalls described are obvious but can still happen when one is in a rush or during a negligent moment.

On the other hand, some pitfalls are less obvious and require a constant awareness. The aim of this chapter is to list the common pitfalls and to show how they can be prevented. All the points of this chapter can form a checklist, allowing those interested to go through it before submitting a project.

VISIBILITY OF LIGHT SOURCES

Light makes everything visible but that doesn't mean that the direct light source needs to be in the line of sight. Good lighting design lives through indirect

Figure 6.01 An example of luminaires unintentionally reflected off glass panels.

Figure 6.02 Jewellery spot lighting approach doesn't work on porcelain.

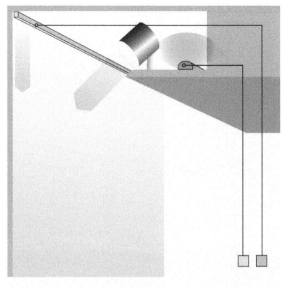

☐ Direct and ☐ indirect lighting out of recess.

Figure 6.03 Two lighting methods in a recess.

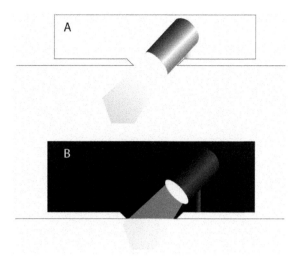

Figure 6.04 A. Shallow, white gorge – Luminaire visible
B. Deep, dark gorge – Luminaire recessed and not visible.

light bouncing off surfaces. It is, of course, all right to see light sources if they are of a decorative nature. A beautiful incandescent or replacement lamp in a restaurant or at home does look appealing. The same applies to pendants, table- and floor-standing lights. When designing, however, within a detail like a niche, slot or cove, the visibility of the actual light source or its reflection is often unwanted. One can distinguish here between two lighting approaches: direct and indirect.

The direct lighting method is more efficient and precise while the indirect method allows for a softer lighting effect. Both have their pitfalls.

Directly lighting out of a recess

Lighting directly out of a recess means one wants to push controlled light into a space or onto an object without major losses. But it also means that the luminaire has to be placed in such a way that it is not visible to the observer. The light has to hit the desired object out of a recess without major loss of the quality of light. Linear lights and spotlights can be used either directly or indirectly in recesses. Spotlights highlight objects while linear lights graze surfaces. Everyone who has played hide and seek as a child knows that it is easier to hide in the dark than in a bright space. It is also easier to disguise oneself in big and busy spaces, but it gets harder to hide in a small location without being quickly spotted.

Consider these possible pitfalls when lighting directly out of recesses.

Direct visibility

Lights or their accessories may be too big and may not fit into the recess. Therefore, the luminaire or one of its components will stick out of the linear cove.

This applies mainly to spotlights in a trough. While the spotlight is allowed to be visible, the other components are not. This might sound obvious but often the luminaires placed into a recess come with additional accessories like tracks, brackets, louvres or drivers. They must also be placed into the recess and that is when it gets tight. A black matte painted cove hides all black lighting components well even when placed visibly into a slot. Any lighter-coloured linear cove, however, requires a good interior finish and all additional components to be hidden. When detailing

Figure 6.05 Spotlights are deep recessed, not visible and organized in group as it should be. Dolce and Gabbana. (Arch: Carbondale; Lighting: Mindseye; Photo: Antoine Huot)

a recess, one must consider that all components required have to fit into the space provided. If the space gets too tight, one should think about placing the necessary driver remotely if possible. If there is not enough space in the recess, the specification needs to change to accommodate all elements. If this isn't possible, one has to negotiate a change of detail with either the architect or the interior designer.

Visibility due to view angle

The light source may be visible due to the view angle. When standing in front of a wall treated with light, the light source in the ceiling/wall cove is not visible yet when one is standing almost parallel to the wall it is.

A detail has to work from all view angles. It is crucial to think how the luminaire will be positioned. It is almost inevitable for the light to be visible if the slot light is positioned on a corner, for example. The same applies to a very long wall and a wide slot.

The questions to be asked is: 'Is the fixture visible if one stands almost parallel to the wall looking directly into the slot?' Depending on the situation, one should consider the following solutions:

1. Changing the detail and making the slot narrower and deeper will make it considerably easier to hide the light grazing directly down a vertical.

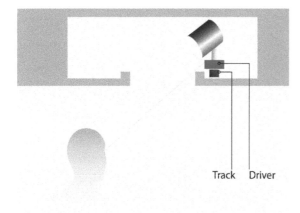

Track   Driver

Figure 6.06 Track lifts the driver over the visibility edge

Figure 6.07 Luminaire not visible when standing in front.

Figure 6.08 Luminaire visible when standing on the corner.

2. Introducing louvres often helps to disguise direct light. The luminaire might still be visible but will not stand out as the direct light source is hidden.
3. If neither of the two previous solutions are feasible due to a low recess depth one can choose a nice-looking light source. This can help one to live with the fact that at some point the light will be visible.

Indirect visibility/reflection

Light may be visible in reflection as a reflective material exposes a recessed light source. Light placed discreetly to highlight the texture or material of a wall may get highlighted by its own reflection. There are two causes of reflection: a single reflective surface and two reflective surfaces. The latter makes it impossible to hide the light within the recess without it being visible on the reflective surface. Lighting surrounded by two reflective surfaces is only possible in a cove with the light not pointing at the surfaces but onto a third matte surface. With a single reflective surface, it

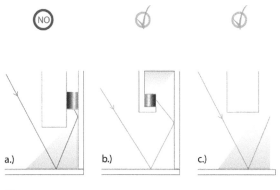

☐ Reflective surface

Figure 6.09
a.) Visible: The second vertical reflective surface reveals the light
b.) Not visible: Cove + luminaire away from the reflective surface.
c.) Single reflective surface - deep recess.

doesn't get much easier. For a light source not to be visible on the reflective surface the slot in the detail has to be very deep to hide a recessed luminaire.

Alternatively, the light can be pointed away from the reflective surface. Louvres and glare shields can help to avoid the visibility of the light source. The impact of the light onto the polished surface has to be tested in any case. Plain glass or a highly polished stone, for example, are unforgiving and will mirror

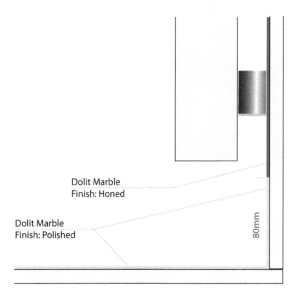

Dolit Marble
Finish: Honed

Dolit Marble
Finish: Polished

80mm

Figure 6.10 Indicate clearly the material change and its dimensions.

Figure 6.11 Handrail lighting not visible - the reflective marble made it difficult to hide the integral linear luminaire. (Photo: Antoine Huot)

Figure 6.12 Lighting calculation of wall washers. a.) Covering part of the wall only. b.) While the right image shows full coverage.

the light precisely. Other reflective materials can show a distorted reflection of the light that in some cases does look acceptable. It is important in any case to get a sample of the material and test the effect with both the original light source and the material. If, for some reason, the proposed measures to prevent reflections are not possible, one has to negotiate with the architect to make the material on the areas where the luminaire will be reflected matte. In this case it is essential that the architect and the lighting designer clearly communicate in their drawings in what areas the change of material treatment has to take place.

SURFACE OR OBJECT COVER

Partial coverage

A light beam may leave the recess and not cover the object or a wall fully. This is a simple task that has to

be checked every time. In an ideal world, a test with the light source can prevent some areas remaining in darkness. But what if I do not have the light source at hand or I am not sure what beam angle to use? In this case, a quick light-beam check in CAD can help, as explained in Chapter 5. Alternatively, a lighting calculation is useful.

Both actions are worthwhile as they allow one to check the light distribution and help to establish the samples needed. In summary, one can say that there are two theoretical ways of checking the beam angle, besides a practical way. The practical way is necessary to establish the quality of the light coverage. This method is usually used to confirm the effect of light grazing a wall. The theoretical ways, on the other hand, are used to establish or confirm the beam angles. They allow one to confirm, for example, a spotlight type and the quantity of lights necessary to illuminate an area.

Shadow gaps

When wall-grazing and bleeding one should make sure one gets a continuously lit surface, with no shadow in the middle or at the end. There are two main reasons for shadow gaps to occur:

1. The linear fittings do not cover the full length of the surface to be lit, therefore, the ends are left in

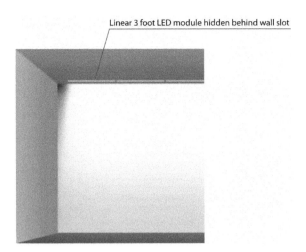

Linear 3 foot LED module hidden behind wall slot

Figure 6.13 Unwanted shadow at the end.

is that the linear lights used do not allow a seamless end-to-end mounting. The distance between the two linear lights is too big. The light escaping the slot doesn't have the space to overlap. When it leaves the slot, these areas are darker. The solution to this is a deeper recess as it allows the light to overlap before it exits the recess. If a deeper recess is not possible, one has to use linear LED fixtures that allow an end-to-end mounting and do not create shadows when butted up against each other.

Light cones

relative darkness. Many linear luminaires come in standard sizes – usually in 1–4ft (30–120cm) increments. The wall might have a dimension that does not allow exact coverage with the specified luminaires. One must make sure the total length of luminaires covers the full length including the two ends. A respecification is necessary if the luminaires combined don't allow end-to-end coverage.

2. A continuous light grazing the wall is interrupted by a dark area. The reason for this unwanted effect

The light may end with a cone on an adjacent wall. The light cone is probably less prominent and noticed than other pitfalls but nevertheless should be avoided if possible. When linear light finishes close to a wall, it creates a strong visible beam of light on the wall.

This can be avoided by making sure the light ends a certain distance from the wall. The ideal distance to the wall varies and depends on the light sources used. If possible, it should be established with a little mock-up.

Figure 6.14 Unwanted shadow where luminaires are joined.

Figure 6.15 Unwanted light cone on the wall.

Figure 6.16 Light can reveal imperfections.

Figure 6.17 LED doesn't have time to mix to a uniform white light.

Surface quality

Your illuminated surface may not look good. Whether to light a surface or not depends on the quality and the finish of the surface. A plain plaster surface, i.e., without an image, requires a perfect and smooth finish. Any unevenness, marks and bumps are highlighted by the light.

The same applies to unattractive tiles with wide joint fillers. One can compare lighting here with makeup. Skin imperfections can be covered by foundation; the lighting design solution is to leave the imperfections in darkness. Attractive features, on the other hand, can be emphasized with makeup – in our case, we use lighting.

Light colour

Your white light may not be consistent, therefore, the surface is not washed in a unifying white light.

We have learned about the definition of MacAdam steps in LEDs. These days, many manufacturers guarantee a light fixture within two MacAdam steps' tolerance. This should in theory guarantee an even white light onto a surface. The surprise can be big when testing the lights; each LED may emit a different white. When holding the light into a slot against a surface at a distance, the light may appear even. This is because the light mixes into a single white light. This mixed white light is within two MacAdam steps accurate to any other light fixture from this manufacturer. Not so each single LED within the luminaire. The MacAdam steps of each LED can vary up to five or more steps and allow these luminaires to be more cost-effective. The pitfall occurs when the fixture is positioned too close to a surface and the ceiling line. The light escaping each single LED does not have the space to mix well.

The distance of these fixture from the wall and the recess must be correct. They cannot be used in areas where their light source is directly visible, or the recess space is too restricted.

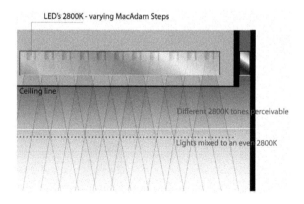

Figure 6.18 The right recess of a linear luminaire from ceiling line to avoid white-inconstancy.

Figure 6.19 Unwanted shadow pattern on the wall.

Light stripes

Light may leave a slot in stripes. When light has to graze up or down a high wall one relies on LEDs with an extremely narrow beam angle.

Linear fixtures are actually LEDs lined up in a strand. Rather than using continuous LED strips, they use single high-power LEDs with a narrow beam angle joined in a line. Each LED is equipped with a narrow lens, i.e., ten by ten degrees. They are mounted onto a PCB board with a certain pitch. The stripes on the wall occur when the light source is mounted too close to a wall and ceiling line in relation

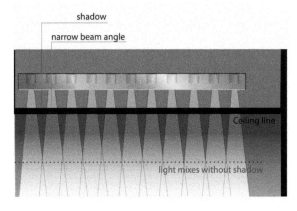

Figure 6.20 The right recess of a linear luminaire from ceiling line to avoid white-inconstancy.

to the LED pitch. The light of each LED does not have the space to mix.

This means that the LED pitch dictates the position of the fixture within the detail. A mock-up is essential to establish the right position of the specified luminaire. If the necessary detail depth isn't available, one has to specify a linear LED with asymmetric lenses i.e. fifteen by sixty degrees. These lenses have a very narrow perpendicular beam angle and a wider parallel beam spread that mix the light onto the wall much sooner. Bear in mind that the asymmetric light will not reach as far down a wall as a ten by ten-degree fixture.

INDIRECTLY LIGHTING OUT OF A RECESS

Lighting indirectly out of a coffer or recess means one wants to create a pleasant diffused light effect. The luminaire has to be disguised, creating either a strong indirect ambient light or a soft indirect linear light glow. Using chunky fluorescent tubes proved very challenging in earlier days but from 2012 things have become much easier with the introduction of compact LED technology. The space necessary to create light gaps and coffers has decreased significantly since then. However, the new LED technology has its own trickiness to consider. Depending on detail and material, there are various pitfalls to bypass when lighting indirectly.

Light shadow

The up-lighting may show a defined shadow edge. Whether up-lighting onto a ceiling or any other surface, one wants a smooth graduation of light. The light should fade gently away rather than stopping abruptly.

The cause of shadowing is an LED placed either too deep or too close to the cove edge. The edge upstand creates an unwanted shadow on the surface

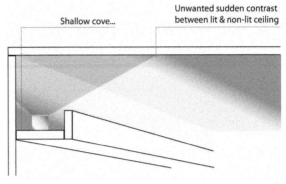

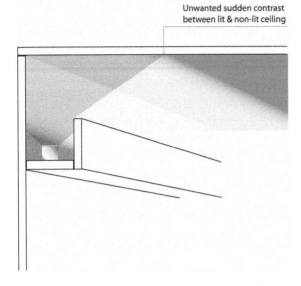

Figure 6.21 The light of the LED is cut by cove ledge, creating a strong shadow rather than smooth graduation.

Figure 6.22 The light of a linear LED doesn't have space to gradually fade.

when hit by the light emitted by the linear LED. By using shallow cove profiles, one can avoid shadowing. Where shallow cove profiles are not possible one should make sure the linear LED fixtures are positioned so the light does not hit the cove edge. This can either be established with a CAD drawing showing the beam angle of the light source or by testing the luminaire within a mock-up.

Light image

The up-lighting may not fade smoothly. Fluorescent lamps emit light in all directions, creating a nice diffused light effect as light bounces off all surfaces within a cove. One gets a smooth fade of light on the lit surface. Achieving the same with a linear LED proves more difficult. Placing a linear LED upwards and simply hoping for the best isn't enough in most cases. Linear LEDs have a defined beam angle based on their design. The beam angle in most linear strip LED is 120 degrees. The linear LED's light cuts off differently, depending on its design. A very shallow cove will reveal the cut-off of a linear LED shining indirectly against a surface.

In many cases, the light stops abruptly, leading to an unwanted quick change between the light and dark areas. The more distance the light has from the surface, the better. In the following image, for example, the light has enough space to diffuse and fade.

If the cove is shallow, one should use linear LEDs with a nice, smooth cut-off angle. They come with a diffuser softening the light cut. The tilting of the light source can create a similar effect. The light has space to fade out naturally. In this case, the back of the cove will not receive any light and will appear dark. This might not be a disadvantage if the back of the cove is a dark material or not visible.

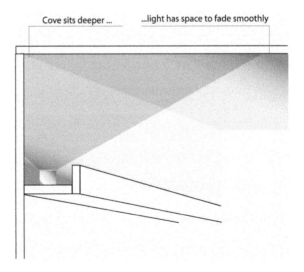

Figure 6.23 A good distance of the cove to the wall, but the defined beam angle of the luminaire creates a shadow on the ceiling.

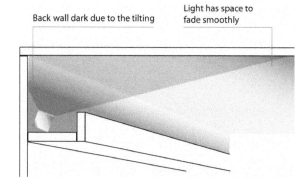

Back wall dark due to the tilting   Light has space to fade smoothly

Figure 6.24 Tiltable uplights within the coffer allow us to correct the light beam direction if necessary.

Figure 6.25 A well-lit coffer using tiltable linear LED – standard 120 degrees.

One can use LEDs with beam angles of 180 degrees or more. They guarantee almost in all cases a good light image on surfaces. This brings us to the colour of the cove. The lighter the colour inside the more light bounces out of the cove. If the cove is deep, it relies on the light bouncing within the cove. In this case, is important to make sure that the drawings specify all inner cove surfaces to be painted matt white.

Corner irregularities

The corner in a coffer may either be too bright or darker than the other areas.

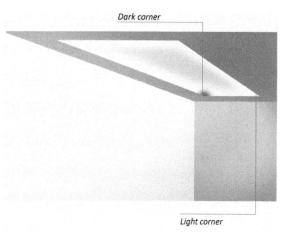

Dark corner

Light corner

Figure 6.26 A coffer showing unwanted dark and bright light-corners.

With fluorescent tubes there was a set of rules to be applied when they were used in coves. This does not apply for LEDs anymore. Depending on their emitted beam angle, type and detail the set-up can vary significantly. The general rule here is that one linear LED starts where the other, usually perpendicular, linear LED finishes. This creates the right amount of light for the corner. This might change if, for example, the distance of the LED to the wall or ceiling is not sufficient. In this case, the LED has to finish earlier to avoid an over-lit corner. The opposite is the case if the distance to the wall is too great or the beam angle of a linear LED is narrower than usual.

In this case, one has to add light in the corner by, for example, extending and crossing the linear lamps. Thanks to the compact dimensions of LEDs, coves have become smaller; at the same time, lighting them correctly has become harder. Each LED type needs a little mock-up to test its performance.

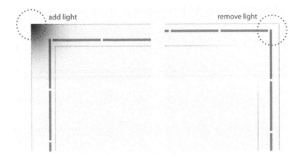

Figure 6.27 Topview of lighting in a ceiling coffer.

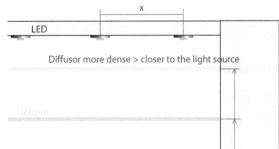

Figure 6.29 Section through a back lit panel with Linear or Dot LEDs layed out in a grid = x. Diffuser at different distances.

LUMINOUS SURFACES

Backlighting: dotting or visible lines

A backlit surface may show a lamp image in the form of dots or lines. Backlighting a stretched ceiling panel or etched glass allows one to push a lot of light evenly into a space. The image one expects of the backlit panel is an evenly lit surface. Lamp imaging is unwanted and happens when the distance of the light source to the diffusing surface is too short. The light from each light source hasn't got the space to overlap before hitting the diffusing surface. If the light sources are linear LED strips then lines will show.

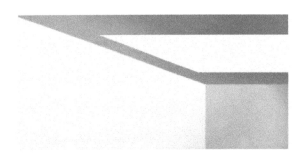

Figure 6.28 Linear shadows visible on the backlit panel.

If one uses LED boards for backlighting, lamp images of dots can occur. The further the light source is away from the backlit surface the fewer lamps are necessary to achieve an evenly backlit surface. If the space is scarce, one has to use more but less intense LED modules to achieve the same light effect. The distance depends further on the

backlit material. An opal glass or stretched membrane will be fairly forgiving.

Therefore, light sources can be placed further away from each other and closer to the diffusor. A more efficient opaque glass, on the contrary, will reveal the light sources more obviously. The lamps must therefore be positioned closer to each other to avoid lamp imaging. For the LED PCB board, this means that the LED pitch needs to be shorter. If the space is too shallow, backlighting become inefficient as it requires the usage of too many lights to guarantee an evenly backlit surface.

Edge-lighting: hot spots, dots and weak light

Light sources may be visible on the edge-lit surface. Edge-lit panels are mostly used in furniture and are integrated. The etched or foiled glass is lit by an LED strip from one or more sides. LEDs will typically show

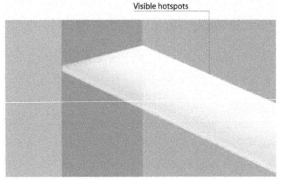

Figure 6.30 Hotspots.

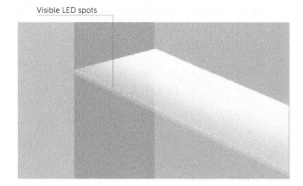

Visible LED spots

Figure 6.31 LED dots are visible on a polished glass edge.

Figure 6.32 Glass as reflector.   Figure 6.33 Glass reveals.

a hot spot of light on the first 30–50mm (1.2–2in) of etched glass.

One has to make sure the first 30mm (1.2in) are covered and thus do not expose the hot spots. The other detail to consider is visible dots if the glass edges are exposed and diffused. The thing to bear in mind is that dots from the LED strips will be visible on the flat polished glass edges.

If not detailed properly, the effect on the edge-lit glass can be weak. To guarantee a good effect, one has to use deep-recessed high-power linear LED strips and, if necessary, lensed LEDs. The achieved effect will never be an evenly lit surface but a nice gradient of light. As one can see, there are many things to consider when it comes to edge lighting, therefore, companies have specialized in manufacturing edge-lit panels. Covered with a diffused glass from above and with the edges sealed these provide an easy solution and guarantee an almost plain lit surface.

THE NATURE OF GLASS

Glass = mirror

We have spoken about reflection but in the world of lighting the window needs special attention. Many tend to forget that glass not only allows light to pass through it but also that it reflects light very well. At night, this effect becomes even more prominent.

All rules that apply to reflective material also apply to glass.

What needs to be considered in addition is that glass exposes all lighting details when viewed from outside. This is not a problem if the building faces a wall or the glass is partly cladded. Otherwise one has to design the lighting details not only to work from the inside but also when viewed from the outside. This means one has to make sure no luminaires are visible and nobody is exposed to glare from them.

Internal light vs external light

Open as usual or closed? Even though this book is dedicated to internal lighting the lighting design of an interior space has an effect on the exterior observer. It is essential, for example, for shops and lobbies to signal that they are open for business. But in some cases, they don't appear open. The space appears dark even though all products within the shop are well lit. The most common reason for this misconception is that surfaces facing the exterior are not being lit sufficiently. The internal space competes with the outside daylight. Dark surfaces are not visible through

Figure 6.34 Unlit surface behind glass.

Figure 6.35 Lit surface behind glass.

Figure 6.37 Unlit garden, exterior visible.

Figure 6.38 Lit garden, exterior visible.

the reflective glass in daylight. As a result, the space appears unused.

Therefore, one must always make sure that the vertical surfaces are lit. Talk to the architect about this necessity. If the walls are not used as displays or don't have a finish that deserves lighting treatment, make sure that this is understood, and the architect can address this issue.

External light vs internal light

It's all dark outside, and where is my beautiful garden? What applies for the interior in daylight also applies to the exterior space in the night-time. A dark garden or courtyard is not visible through a window of a lit reception room. The reflection of lit interior space in the window prevents one from seeing anything that is outside. Often, outdoor lighting is not part of the budget, and if this is so all parties should be made aware of it. It is helpful to allow for some budget for the lighting of the exterior space.

Figure 6.36 Most verticals are treated showing that BMW Park Lane is 'open for business'.

Figure 6.39 Shopwindow lighting not able to compete with bright exterior sunlight.

Figure 6.40 Shop window is perceived as to bright compared to the dark exterior.

Shop windows

A shop window may appear too dark or too bright. A shop window allows the viewer to conclude the relationship between exterior and interior. Shop windows are small, exterior-facing spaces and are therefore exposed to constant changes in light level throughout a day. The outer light level can vary between 10 lux and 30,000 lux. This means that the light inside needs to be powerful enough to be noticed throughout the day but at the same time not be too bright in the night-time. It is essential to allow for a lot of light in a shop window when the light outside is very bright

For the evening hours, bright shop window lights must be dimmed. For eyes that are used to a dark evening light level, shop window illumination can easily become too bright.

What applies generally to the interior space of a shop also applies to shop windows. One has to make sure the vertical surfaces are lit to set a background to the scene and create visibility.

MIRROR, MIRROR ON THE WALL...

Light exposed

Light or untidy detail may be visible though a mirror or polished metal. When designing with details in front

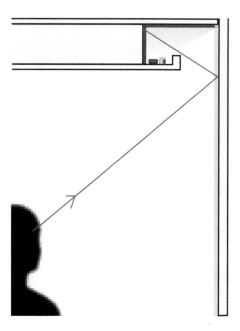

Figure 6.41 Keep the cove tidy – the mirror reveals all.

of mirrors, one has to bear in mind that depending on the mirror position the light source in a cove, for example, may be fully visible. It is not only the luminaire but also the inner surfaces of the cove that will

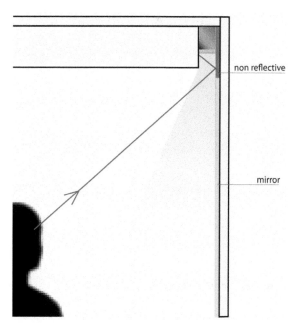

non reflective

mirror

Figure 6.42 Shorten the mirror to avoid visibility or use a nice linear if you can't.

be exposed by a mirror. The same rule applies here as with details located beside glass. The detail must be designed and built bearing full visibility in mind. To avoid visibility, slots by mirrors are narrow and deep.

Accessing a luminaire isn't always easy. This means that it is much harder to make and keep a detail by a mirror visually tidy.

One has to allow for enough space for the electrician to keep the detail tidy by placing the lights out of sight and hiding the drivers if there is no opportunity to keep them remotely. If this proves difficult, one can alternatively use linear fixtures in a deep recess. Diffused linear luminaires are designed to be visible and will deliver more light downwards compared to indirect light.

Alternatively, if a wider slot is needed to provide more light downwards, it might be worth having a talk with the interior designers. In this case, it will be useful to make the mirror shorter to avoid reflection. A few centimetres can help to prevent the luminaire being seen in the mirror. It might help to do a quick check in CAD as shown in Chapter 5 to establish the ideal mirror height and thus avoid the visibility of the light source.

Unflattering light

We have surely all experienced it – when looking at our own reflection in the mirror we don't look always favourable. In front of some mirrors we look good, while others make us appear disadvantageous. This isn't down to the magic mirror but to good or bad lighting. We have learned in Chapter 2 about the properties of various luminaires. A down-light with a defined beam angle placed directly over a mirror, for example, creates a crisp and contrast-filled light. This type of light is suitable for bringing out the best in beautiful objects, but on our faces it will cast stark shadows, and reveal spots and wrinkles. One solution to this pitfall is to use a diffused light source. The aim is to create a soft light not exposing irregularities and creating more even illumination. Linear details

providing diffused light are a good solution. When using detail beside mirrors as a main light source one has to make sure there is sufficient light on the person standing in front of it. It doesn't always need to be a linear light; it can also be a medium-sized diffused down-light or a big diffused light panel, as they also create a good light by the mirror. If one cannot touch the wall or ceiling one can position the light behind the mirror, creating a diffused indirect up-light. This works particularly well in lower spaces. Alternatively, a surface-mounted diffused light source is a good solution. The luminaire market offers plenty of good decorative and architectural diffused wall-mounted luminaires. And last but not least, don't forget that mirror is a glass with a silver back-foil. If there is space, one can use partially etched mirror glass to deliver light from behind the glass.

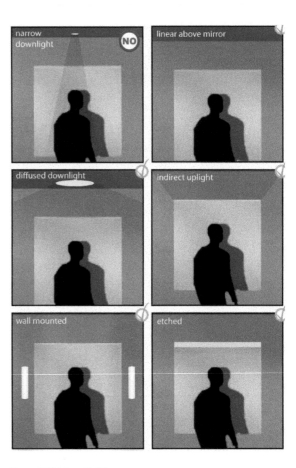

Figure 6.43 Mirror lighting.

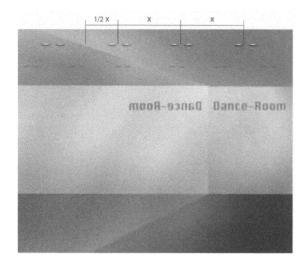

Figure 6.44 Mirror lighting continues seamless into the mirror.

Keep the rhythm

Ones rhythm may be interrupted. Mirrors are used in architecture to make spaces appear bigger. When placing down-lights into a space one also has to consider what the effect will be on the mirror, especially when one has an array of down-lights crossing a space up to the mirror. To support this effect of a visually larger space, one should place the last light of the array at the right distance from the wall. The intention is to make the down-lights appear as if they would continue naturally into the mirror. This is best achieved by placing the last down-light by the mirror at half the distance it has from the other down-lights.

THE LUMINAIRE IN THE SPACE

Layers are key

There may be something missing but what? A good lighting scheme completes the good design of a space. What it cannot do is make average architecture look outstanding. A soulless lighting scheme, however, can ruin a space. All details may be working well, and there may be no glare, but the space still feels wrong. This is often down to incorrect lighting. Some

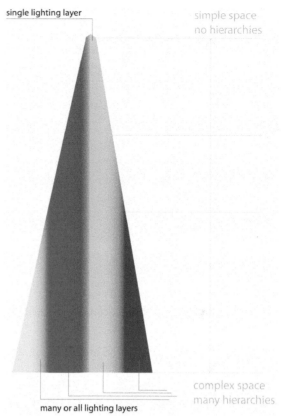

single lighting layer · simple space no hierarchies

many or all lighting layers · complex space many hierarchies

Figure 6.45 The relationship of layer versus hierarchy and space complexity.

lighting schemes fail to address either architectural elements or vertical surfaces. Other schemes are too contrasting and general light is missing or overused. For example, using general light also as task light leads to a dull and uniformly lit space. Using only task lights can create uncomfortable contrast and will not provide sufficient light in other areas. The reason for unsuccessful lighting is often a lack of layers or too many layers of light. Make sure you use layers according to the space. A simple corridor, for example, won't require too many layers. An accent light illuminating the wall can supply sufficient general light yet accentuate the wall at the same time. A hotel lobby, on the other hand, will usually need all lighting layers from general light, accent light and task light to decorative light. A balanced scheme is a lighting scheme that respects the hierarchy of the space by the number of layers it uses.

The pendant

Light may be hanging too high or too low. Pendant luminaires form an important sector of decorative luminaires. Equally important are the technical pendants, which can provide, for example, combined up- and down-light for a space. When up-lighting is part of the provided luminaire feature, one must make sure that there is sufficient space between the luminaire's up-lighting light source and the ceiling. The light needs the room to bounce off the ceiling into the space. The light is mounted too high when the up-light creates a narrow line of light on the ceiling. It not only looks unappealing but it isn't efficient either as a lot of the light will hit the pendant rather than continuing its journey toward the table. The other pitfall is if the light hangs too low. The lower the light is positioned, the weaker the effect of the upward light is, as the light has to travel more.

The ideal distance of a technical light from the ceiling depends again on the beam angle of the up-light and should be tested or sourced from the lighting manufacturer. The ideal rule of position for decorative pendants is 'not in the way and

Figure 6.47 Pendant suspended in the right height. (Arch: AHMM)

Figure 6.46 Pendant up-downlight.

not out of sight'. With 'not in the way', one means the luminaire should not be visually and physically obstructive. With 'not out of sight', one means that it should be positioned to still perform its purpose by visually enhancing a space.

The right size

Lighting may feel too big or too small within the space. The integration of luminaires into a detail defines the size of the luminaires. So does the design of a space – it not only dictates the type but also the dimensions of the luminaires.

It can happen that a 1m (3.3ft) light panel looks lost and small in a 10m- (32.8ft-) high hotel reception, while the 200mm (7.9in) down-light in a corridor is perceived as large in dimension.

Figure 6.49 Different zones in a house compared. The staircase, office desk and kitchen top are perceived brightly even though the Lux level figures are 'low'.

Figure 6.48 Left. 1.5metre luminaire in a massive space. Right. 200mm luminaire in a small corridor.

As general rule, one can establish that small fixtures are suitable for small or low rooms while higher and bigger rooms are more forgiving with bigger luminaires. As with many things, the exception proves the rule, such as a big diffused light at the end of a corridor or an array of small luminaires, creating a cluster of lights in a lobby. This brings us to the quantity and position of luminaires.

Lack of contrast

There may be too much light. We have talked in Chapter 3 about how to lay out and group luminaires in a space to create a base light level. A lighting calculation can be helpful to check the general light level, but it can also be misleading. The false colour imaging exaggerates the not-so-bright areas. In a false colour image, 50 lux can look dark, but in many cases it might be more than enough. To establish whether the lux level is sufficient, a lux meter might be of help for the unexperienced. Measure your office environment and you will soon find out that what you

thought is dark might actually be an acceptable light level. Checking the environment with a lux meter helps to re-tune one's perception. The mistake one often encounters is that the base light is too high. It is often ignored that light needs contrast to make objects stand out. Too much light is used when there is no notable rhythm between accentuated lighting and generally lit space. It is of course possible to dim the lights to correct over-lighting. But what if that many lights weren't necessary at all? Knowing when and where to omit lights requires some experience, courage or the lux meter in the office.

The right amount

Having too many luminaires or falling in love with a particular luminaire can be an issue. Having a lot of light in a room doesn't necessarily mean that there are many visible light fixtures. One can provide a lot of light in a space by using various lighting tools. The luminaires in the space shouldn't overpower visually but blend in nicely. To achieve general light, task light

Figure 6.50 Top-heavy - single luminaire usage.

Figure 6.51 Balanced - mixed luminaire usage.

achieve a lighting scheme with ones favourite fixtures but with the right tools. The aim is to arrange a composition of luminaires to accomplish the right lighting for the space without letting one luminaire type dominate it visually.

The right distance and size

Grouped down-lights may be set at the wrong distance. Most manufacturers define the position of their wallwasher down-lights from the wall and from each other in their catalogues and web pages. We assume that everybody reads and obeys this recommendation. There is not much space for creativity and to play here. We have spoken in Chapter 3 about grouping the lights and how to organize the ceiling. Defining the distance between the grouped down-lights can sometimes prove difficult. The different light fixtures in a group can be either too far apart or too close to each other. If the down-lights are adjustable, it doesn't affect the light quality and is therefore often neglected. It does, however, affect the visual appearance of the space. There is a quick

Figure 6.52 Test: paper cut-outs of 60mm and 150mm laid out onto the floor.

and accent light using only one type of light fixture yet having a balanced luminaire arrangement is hard to accomplish. One needs a lot of down-lights, for example, to generate all three lighting layers. In a confined space, the usage of many down-lights will make the ceiling appear crowded. As we know, variety is the spice of life so removing some of the down-lights using wall slots can calm the ceiling visually. The reason for using too many luminaires of one kind can be varied. We might get to a point where we have our favourite manufacturer or light fixture. But that doesn't mean that this luminaire deserves a space in a lighting scheme. One should not aim to method to check the right distance. Print and cut out circles in the size of the down-lights. Put them on the floor and play with the distance until it looks all right. This applies not only to adjustable lights but also to standard down-lights or grouped linears. This method is not only helpful for establishing the distance between luminaires but also when it comes to defining their size. One can discover using this method that the lights are too big or small when laying them out physically.

Missed target

Adjustable luminaires are often used as a miracle cure. They are tempting as they allow one to adjust the lighting when things on site change. They are also used when the design for a space remains unclear at the time the lighting design is taking place. Due to their functionality, good adjustable down-lights look slightly different to regular down-lights. They are bigger if they allow for good adjustability. Adjustable down-lights that look like standard down-lights have a very limited adjustability. The main pitfall with adjustables is that they may not reach the target even though one has checked it in a CAD drawing. We have shown how to define the position of an adjustable down-light in Chapter 5. The pitfall lays in the actual adjustability of the luminaire. To the lighting designer's misfortune, some manufacturers do not mention in their information sheets that the beam angle of their product is compromised at maximum tilt. This is especially the case with the small deep-recessed adjustable down-lights. Their shape doesn't allow the light to physically escape the cylindrical recess. The maximal tilting angle of the lamp might be twenty degrees while the actual escape angle is only ten degrees.

These are beautiful little fixtures, but the beauty comes at a price. They are nevertheless a favourite fixture with many lighting designers. If designers decide to keep the specification of a deep-recessed small down-light, they must be aware of the limitations of the fixture and use it accordingly. The

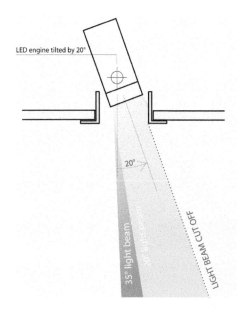

Figure 6.53 Light beam obstructed and cut to half

same applies to some pinhole adjustables. Pinhole adjustable downlights have the right design, allowing the light to be moved into the right position. Their mechanism allows for precise tilting but once the faceplate is put back one discovers that it cuts off some of the light beam. The price to be paid for a good functioning adjustable down-light is its bigger size.

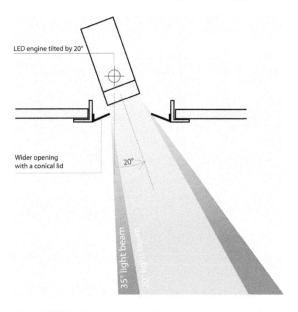

Figure 6.54 Light beam escaping without obstruction through a pinhole.

Adjustable down-lights need to be tested for full functionality before being specified. If none of the envisaged adjustables are suitable even though they are fully adjustable, moving them might be the only option.

Stairs and landings

There may be an issue with glare on the stairs. Stairs are particularly hard to illuminate. A position of a luminaire or detail that works perfectly in a normal space might not be suitable on stairs. Simple down-lighting, for example, is sometimes not possible as the geometry of the space is too complex. It is often not possible to use ceilings to place a luminaire. The stair above might be in its way or the ceilings may simply not be horizontal. A carelessly placed down-light on an angled ceiling can cause glare to a person walking down the stairs.

Even a floor-washer can, when not placed properly, cause glare. A stair can have two vertical surfaces – the inner and the outer surface. If a wall-mounted floor-washer is positioned on the outer vertical surface, glare can occur under some conditions when walking up the stairs.

If possible, one should place floor-washers on the inner side of the staircase. A person, whether walking

Figure 6.56 Walking up or down the stairs – outer luminaires perceived more.

upwards or downwards, is more likely to look towards the outer side of stairs. It also keeps the staircase visually cleaner.

Stair illumination can also be delivered via a lighting detail. Whether under-handrail or under-step lighting, the visibility in staircases is high. A staircase can create various unusual viewpoints. This allows one to look into details that would normally not be exposed. With this in mind, details need to be planned even more carefully. Viewpoints must be checked in 2D CAD drawings or, even better, in 3D CAD models if available. One should avoid linear LEDs where dots are visible but rather use opal diffused linear LEDs as it is most likely that the light source is visible.

From above

One may see the light fixture, including the cabling, from above. Standard details are designed to work in normal room geometry. Light fixtures and accessories are exposed the moment the room geometry changes and new higher- or lower-view angles appear.

One has to be cautious and consider this new viewpoint. For example, cabling in a cove or an edge lighting will be visible when observed from above.

Figure 6.55 Glare caused by staircase lighting.

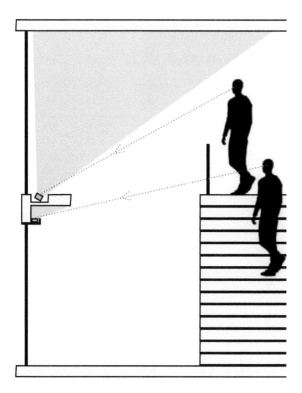

Figure 6.57 High level position allows to look into otherwise hidden lighting details.

Typical architectural elements that should make the alarm bells ring when working on a detail are: stairs and their landings, bridges, floor openings and terraces. The design must consider that the light sources will be fully visible. If possible, the luminaires used should be architectural luminaires. Architectural luminaires have integral drivers and cables that can be hidden. The alternative is to use technical luminaires and cover them either with an opal sheet or hide them behind louvres and a glare shield. All finishes have to be good with a light source either not visible or creating a good level of diffusion. The level of detail depends on the distance to the exposed detail – the further away, the more forgiving. When designing the detail, one must establish the visibility line. Louvres and a shield must be used with light sources that have a defined beam angle used for washing or grazing. A diffuser would change the light completely and can't be used with grazers and washers. The louvres and shield need to be positioned to not obstruct the beam angle and to hide the light from view. An attractive architectural light or an opal cover should be used when a simple diffused up-light is needed.

The dark side

A corner, niche or space may be left in darkness. Contrast is an important part of lighting and the dark area is equally as important as the bright part of a space. One can illuminate a space perfectly with the right contrast between lit and unlit areas, yet sometimes areas are left out. This is not unusual and can happen with complex spaces. One should, in particular, pay attention to the underside of an ending of staircases.

Very often, these areas appear dark and forgotten in an otherwise well-lit space. A little glow is often enough to bring them into presence without giving them too much importance. The same applies to niches and corners. The reason these spaces are forgotten is because they are not accessed, they don't have a function and are not in a major pathway. Lights are easily hidden in such spaces. The lighting doesn't need to be sophisticated as they won't be directly visible. A cost-effective, simple, surface-mounted light can do a good job. It is rare that the end of a staircase is celebrated with a light panel.

Figure 6.58 Dark areas under stairs deserve a glow.

Figure 6.59 A usually neglected area gets special attention.
(Arch: HOK and Seth Stein; Lighting: Mindseye; Photo: Andy Spain)

CONTROL IS EVERYTHING

Irregularities

You may have a great control system yet some lights are flickering, or the dimming happens only at the last 10 per cent. This is often frustrating. Even though the right control gear has been used with each luminaire, some light sources don't behave as expected. The main reason for the malfunction is that some drivers are not compatible with the control system. To avoid this one should aim to use control gear from the control system manufacturer chosen for the project. All the drivers and gears of the control system manufacturer are optimized to work with its own control units. Alternatively, one can use drivers that have been tested with the selected control system. All good lighting manufacturers are interested in ensuring that their luminaires work with the major lighting control systems. They test their drivers and can guarantee good respond of their equipment. When it is left to the lighting designer to specify drivers, it is important to consult with the control system company about compatibility of the selected drivers. If there are doubts, one should look for alternative drivers.

Synchronization

Two lights on the same circuit may dim differently. Dimming many lights together that are on the same control circuit doesn't automatically mean that they will behave in the same way. Bear in mind that lights that are on one control circuit will get the same control signal, but a down-light, a linear and the joinery lighting run on different drivers. All drivers may react differently to the control signal. There are two solutions to this. If possible, try to separate the lights into control groups. Down-lights should be on a different circuit to joinery lights, etc. This is not always possible due to budget constraints – remember, the more circuits there are, the costlier the scheme gets. In this case, make sure to get drivers from the same family to get similar dimming behaviours.

In practice

You may find that control practice deviates from theory. Once all scenes are set and the project is handed over to the client one should make sure that everyone understands that this is a first set-up. The best practice is to allow the client to live with the scene settings for a while. After some time, the client might have some adjustment requirements. The adjustments reflect the actual needs of the client and how they use the space in their daily life. If necessary, you may require a second session with the technician of the lighting control system to adjust the scenes accordingly.

Switches

Where is the light switch? A modern lighting control system comes with nice wall switches. Despite iPad apps and remote controls, a switch has still its place in a building, and switches may be placed in unusual positions, depending on the design of the space. The main rule is to allow for switches at space entries/exits. If a space is bigger, allow for an additional control point, ideally near the area where the user spends most time in the room. This applies to a bedroom where the light switches should be by the beds. Switches for bathrooms in public places should be inside the bathrooms since there is a lot of traffic, and someone could accidentally turn an outside light off while the bathroom is in use. In residential projects, wall switches can be placed outside the bathrooms.

JOINERY LIGHTING

Most of the aforementioned pitfalls can occur with joinery lighting as well. The same rules apply when it comes to highlighting texture or being careful with reflection and glare. However, joinery lighting deserves a section of its own, in particular with regard to lighting products. It is effectively lighting design for small spaces that are being observed by giants from above. The light distances, light intensities and view angle are different.

Half-lighting

Why is the shelf only half lit? Not using joinery lighting when it is actually necessary is the first pitfall in joinery lighting. Local joinery light gives a product a presence and makes it stand out. It does, however, add to the lighting budget and is therefore not always

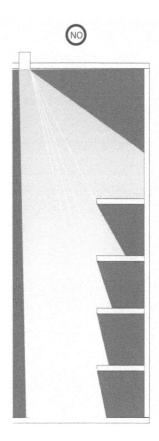

Figure 6.60 Diagram showing that light is not reaching products.

possible. It is best to show all parties involved with a little section diagram why the product cannot be lit from above.

One should consider using joinery lighting if a product isn't fully coverable by ceiling light due to a shelf design or ceiling restriction. A half-lit product must be avoided if possible. If the budget doesn't allow for integration of light, try to change the shelf parameters together with the architect. Otherwise, use joinery lighting where desired and necessary.

Partial coverage

Perhaps a product is lit only partly. Unlike when lighting a space, there are no regulations to comply with for joinery lighting. Ones wellbeing and safety do not rely on joinery lighting. But whether a product sells or doesn't depends partly on lighting. To guarantee a

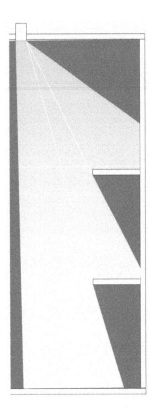

Figure 6.61 Product on the floor not lit well.

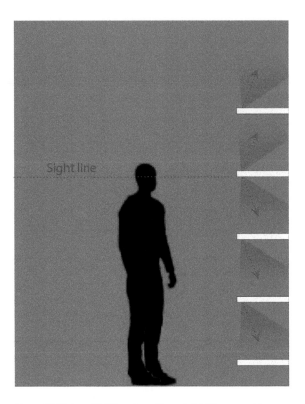

Figure 6.62 Integral lighting above the red sight line cannot be placed under the shelf otherwise it would be visible. The product must be lit from below,

good light level, the same rigor must be applied here as when lighting a space. The distance to the lighting target is less, which leads to much wider beam angles. If spotlights are used, they must cover the product fully. They have to cover it from the front and illuminate the depth.

The best practice is to check the detail in a mock-up. The layout can be applied onto all shelf types in the project after the ideal set-up has been approved. This can be achieved by a beam-spot check on CAD as explained in Chapter 5. This is important for each shelf type and will prevent products being lit only partly.

under the shelf and are therefore disguised by the shelf holding them. But one can do this only up to a certain height. If the shelves are at a 1.7m (5.6ft) height, down-lights start to become visible to some people. At 1.9m (6.2ft), the under-shelf lights are visible to most of us. If the luminaires can't be hidden in a detail from the direct view, one must make sure that shelf lights are installed on the bottom shelf, lighting upwards. When doing a detail for a shelf, one needs to consider the position of the shelves and that a second detail might be necessary.

'Copy paste'

Light sources may be clearly visible in shelves. 'Copy paste' or thoughtless repetition is the main culprit for this pitfall. Lighting down onto a shelf from the shelf above is an easy exercise – the lights are placed

Deep dark

A shelf may appear dark even though the product is on or within lit joinery. As mentioned previously, low, deep shelves are difficult to light fully. One is not able to illuminate them entirely with ceiling luminaires

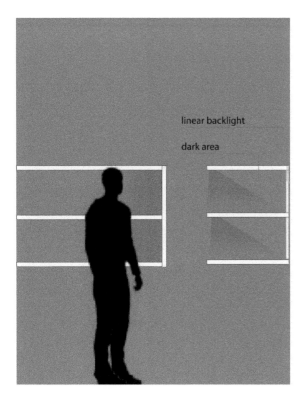

linear backlight

dark area

Figure 6.63 Linear accent light compensating the dark area in the back of the dark shelf.

Figure 6.64 Left side shows backlighting with a light panel. Right side adds front light to the backlight.

only. The last part of the shelf will inevitably look dark and dead. This can be resolved with joinery lighting in most cases. Sometimes even integral lights will struggle to light the deep areas, especially if the shelves are made out of dark material. Why light a shelf fully if the product is already lit? As mentioned before, joinery lighting has to be approached like lighting spaces. In this case, the space is in need of a second layer in the form of an additional light. This can be another point light, or a linear vertical or horizontal light placed at the end of the shelf. The aim is to add a graze or bleed light to invigorate the shelves that would otherwise be perceived as dark.

Appropriate intensity

A shelf may be brightly lit from the back, but the product remains dark. Another method to enliven a shelf is to backlight it with a light panel. The pitfall occurs when the backlighting in the shelves is too strong. The backlight can bathe the entire shelf in a pleasant light and give a nice halo to a product. But one should bear in mind that backlight is not illuminating the product; it provides the secondary layer only. The primary layer, which is the front light, is missing or is not perceived. If the front light is not sensed, this means that the contrast between the light hitting the eye from the light panel and the light bouncing off the product is too high, in favour of the backlighting. Therefore, when planning to use backlight, one should make sure that there is a very strong front light. The key is not making the backlight appear too strong and dominant. The easiest way is to test the effect upfront and change the intensity of the backlight accordingly. If there are many different backlit shelves and the details vary, make sure to set one backlight level for all shelves. Bear in mind that less backlight is more and don't forget that a nice backlight is the secondary layer only.

Stealing the show

Joinery lighting may steal the show in a display. Joinery lighting is mainly used to illuminate a product, keeping the visual impact minimal. If one struggles to integrate lighting into display tables, for example, a good way to light the products is to use LED spotlights on vertical supports.

They are small and deliver the light where needed. But they can steal the show if not carefully used. Be careful when positioning the luminaires as they shouldn't stand in the way. Group the lights by placing two lights together and don't use too many luminaires. This is a good way to reduce their otherwise strong visual presence. Using two lighting poles to light a small ring will be perceived as exaggerated and can be considered stealing the show.

With a group of big watches, on the other hand, one will barely notice the two poles doing their job, providing that the light poles are minimal in design and correspond in material, size and height with their environment.

Type

There may be enough light from the joinery, yet things don't feel right. The type of light used is very important, especially when lighting products. The wrong light either makes the product look too flat or there are too many reflections visible, distracting from the view of the product itself. One has to ask the right questions: is the shelf displaying shoes, leather goods or is it going to show clothes or sunglasses? The general rule is that the majority of products, in particular sparkling and shiny objects, profit from spotlights.

The same applies to textured products as the point

Figure 6.65 Left side: the two display lights steal the show. Right side: one discrete light source.

Figure 6.66 Spotlight highlighting the sparkling stones and the leather structure.

sources emphasize the textures by creating light and shadow. A linear or panel luminaire will distribute diffused, flat light, making the product appear flat. Their strength is to illuminate products with a large reflective surface like sunglasses, smartphones, model cars, etc.

Point sources here would create undesired strong reflections accompanied by indirect glare.

Figure 6.67 Light panel over the BMW create swage line on the car. Spot light are hidden in the slot. (Arch: Carbondale; Lighting: Mindseye; Photo: Andy Spain)

CHANGE OF SPECIFICATION

A change of specification usually occurs between Stage 2 and Stage 3 of the lighting design process, due to design changes. It also can happen during the building process when, due to alteration on site, a specified luminaire doesn't fit physically. This is not necessarily a problem as long as the change of specification is dealt with by the project lighting designer. In some cases, alternative luminaires are proposed by the contractor or the client's project manager due to existing agreements with lighting manufacturers. This is where most pitfalls lie.

Ticking the boxes

The luminaire on site may not be right. One should make sure that all the boxes are ticked when approving a specification change. Make sure the plaster-in/seamless fixture is truly seamless, that the new size is still compatible with the detail and that the beam angle is the same. Check the changes against your specification sheet.

Hidden specification

All boxes may be ticked but still something is not right. When writing a specification, some of the specifications may be particular to a certain luminaire. The lighting designer will be familiar with the specific nature of the fixture, but this may not be noted in the specification sheet. Make sure that an adjustable luminaire retains the same level of adjustability, that the diffused linear that you specified is indeed a linear and that the LED dots are not visible in the new luminaire. This proves difficult if one doesn't have the actual replacement on ones desk. Whenever possible, try to get samples of the alternative luminaire so you can compare its performance with the original specification.

CONCLUSION

There are numerous pitfalls listed in this chapter and they might be overwhelming at the first read. Yet the number has been kept below fifty and to ease understanding they have been separated into sections. The sections and their pitfalls form a checklist shown on the next page. This can be used to verify whether all pitfalls have been considered. It can equally be used as a design guideline or reminder during the design process of each project. Over time, the list will become unnecessary as your project experience and wealth of knowledge about lighting design grows and grows. Good luck!

A CHECKLIST OF POTENTIAL PITFALLS

Recess and space
Is there enough space to hide spotlight and equipment inside a recess? Allow for black finish and recess fixture deep into the cove.

Recess in a corner
Is your recess in a corner? Make sure the luminaire is either deep recessed. Use louvres or nice looking fixtures.

Recess and reflection
A recess against a reflective wall or floor? Point the fixture away from the reflective surfaces.

Wall-washing overall coverage
Is your surface fully covered with light, the graduation smooth? Are there any dark areas?

Wall-grazing lateral coverage
Is your spacing good? Are the ends of the walls covered with light?

Wall-grazing interrupted
Light-shadows on the wall? Do the fixtures allow end to end mounting?

Wall-grazing adjacent wall
Is light escaping onto the other wall? Make sure the wall washing fixtures aren't too close to the adjacent wall.

Wall-grazing – surface quality
Is the wall worth to be treated with light? Make sure the finish and texture of the wall is good. Do not light mirrored or glass surfaces.

Wall-grazing – MacAdam
Make sure your fixture has a MacAdam rating of two or more. If using a linear LED luminaire, make sure the single LEDs have the same MacAdam rating when using to close surfaces.

Wall-grazing – light stripes
When using extreme narrow beam angle to graze a wall, make sure the light has space to mix. Recess the luminaire deeper if necessary.

Cove – light shadow
The up-stand of a cove can cause shadow if the luminaire is placed too close to it. Move the light away from ledges!

Cove – light image
Away from the cove-upstand, still shadow on ceiling? Some luminaires have a sharp light cut-off causing the light to stop abruptly. Make sure the to use a light with a wide beam.

Cove corners
How do the luminaires meet in the corner of the cove? Make sure they are neither too close not too far away from the cove-corner.

Back-lighting
Lamp image visible when back-lighting? Make sure the distance between LEDs and lit surface is right!

Edge-lighting: hot spots
Light hotspots will show the first 30–50mm when edge-lighting. Retrieve the glass by the amount or cover the area of concern.

Edge-lighting: exposed dots
Chamfered polished glass edged will show LED dots. In this case make sure to use LEDs with diffuser.

The nature of glass
Chamfered polished glass edges will show LED dots. Make sure to use LEDs with diffuser.

Glass = mirror!
Hiding luminaires near a window or glass partition in side a cove or trough? Make sure lights are not reflected by the glass. Make sure lights are not visible from outside.

Open for business?
Make sure vertical surfaces are lit if you want visibility from outside.

Shop-window
A shop-window has to work day and night. Make sure the light is sufficient and adaptable.

Mirror – luminaires exposed
Mirror will expose luminaires. Make sure light sources in your detail are not visible.

Mirror – unflattering
Are you using the right light by the mirror? It must be frontal, diffused or indirect. Use soft rather than hard pointlights from above.

Mirror – rhythm
Are you using luminaires in an array close to a mirror? Make sure your layout works with the mirror reflection.

Layers
Are you using your three layers? Is your scheme lacking lighting layers? Do you have too many layers of light?

Pendants
Luminaire hangs too high or too low? The ideal rule for positioning a decorative pendants is 'Not in the way, yet not out of sight'.

Size
Does the size of the fixture suit the size of the space? Small fixtures are suitable for small or low rooms and vice versa.

Lack of contrast
Make sure your general light level isn't too high. Can you create a light contrast of 1:5 or higher if necessary?

The right amount?
Did you fall in love with a fixture? Aim to arrange a composition of luminaires to accomplish the right lighting rather than using your favourite luminaire.

The right distance and size?
Do you know that the size and distance of the luminaires are right? Did you test your arrangement?

Hitting your target?
Did you check whether your adjustable downlight is hitting its target? Make sure you double-check this in a CAD drawing.

Stairs
Stairs and landing allow one to look into details that normally are not exposed. Make sure your luminaires are not visible and do not cause glare.

Alarm bells
Careful with details near stairs, landings, bridges, floor openings and terraces. Details below can be easily looked into. Make sure you check visibility and take action.

Overseen
Are there any niches or staircase endings? If so, make sure they are lit and do not look neglected.

Control irregularities
Make sure drivers are compatible with the control system to avoid flickering or dimming abnormalities when controlling light.

Joinery – half lit
A product isn't fully covered by ceiling light due to shelf design or ceiling restriction. Check via CAD and introduce joinery lighting if necessary.

Joinery – covered by lighting
Is your product on the shelf covered fully by integral joinery lighting? Check it in a mock-up or via CAD drawing.

Joinery – visible from above and below
Not all shelves are equal. The position of the shelf determines whether the integral joinery luminaire is visible from below or from above.

Joinery – deep dark
Is a deep shelf frontally lit? Be careful that you don't only illuminate the front of the shelf. Check it in a Mock-Up or via CAD drawing.

Joinery – back-lit
Is your object back-lit? Make sure your front light is strong enough.

Joinery – proportion
Using pole luminaires? Make sure their size and proportion are right compared with the lit objects.

Joinery – luminaire type
Make sure you use point-lights on shiny and textured objects, and linear or panel luminaires on large reflective surfaces.

Specification change – 1
If another party suggests a specification change, agree only if it matches your original specification in performance.

Specification change – 2
If another party suggests a specification change, don't forget to double-check that the new linear luminaire won't show LED dots if that's not what you want.

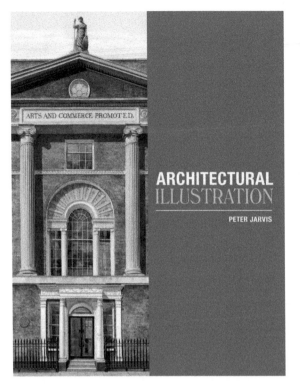

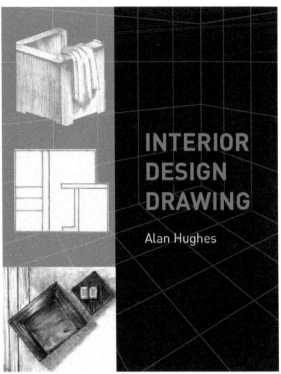

Architectural Illustration 978 1 78500 403 2

Interior Design Drawing 978 1 84797 016 9

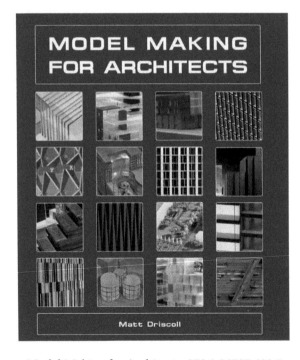

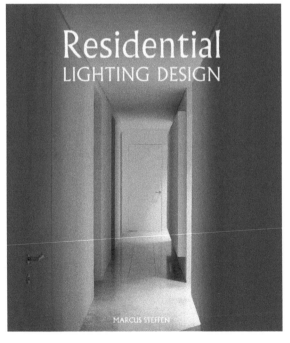

Model Making for Architects 978 1 84797 490 7

Residential Lighting Design 978 1 84797 756 4